CULTURAL POLITICS

Writing Ireland: colonialism, nationalism and culture
David Cairns and Shaun Richards

Poetry, language and politics *John Barrell*

The Shakespeare myth *Graham Holderness*

Garden – nature – language *Simon Pugh*

Teaching women: feminism and English studies
Ann Thompson and Helen Wilcox (editors)

Gender, race, Renaissance drama *Ania Loomba*

Pre-Raphaelites re-viewed *Marcia Pointon (editor)*

Comics: ideology, power and the critics *Martin Barker*

Sha

Me
Sl

Tru
o

Rea
Si

Pos
Jol

Fro
in

The
Yc

Further ti

To Ruth, Laura and Eleanor
For my Mother and Father

The end-of-the-century party

Youth and pop towards 2000

Steve Redhead

with photographs by Kevin Cummins

MANCHESTER UNIVERSITY PRESS
MANCHESTER and NEW YORK

distributed exclusively in the USA and Canada by ST. MARTIN'S PRESS, *New York*

Published by Manchester University Press
Oxford Road, Manchester M13 9PL, UK
and Room 400, 175 Fifth Avenue,
New York, NY 10100, USA

Distributed exclusively in the USA and Canada
by St. Martin's Press Inc.,
175 Fifth Avenue, New York, NY 10010, USA

British Library cataloguing in publication data
Redhead, Steve
The end of the century party: youth and pop towards 2000. — (Cultural politics).
1. Popular music. Social aspects
I. Title II. Series
780'.42

Library of Congress cataloging in publication data
Redhead, Steve
The end-of-the-century party: youth and pop toward 2000 / Steve Redhead
p. cm. — (Cultural politics)
Includes bibliographical references.
ISBN 0-7190-2826-4 — ISBN 0-7190 2827-2 (pbk.)
1. Popular music — 1981 — History and criticism. 2. Popular culture.
I. Title. II. Series.
ML3470.R43 1990
306.4'84—dc20 89-13278

ISBN 0 7190 2826 4 *hardback*
0 7190 2827 2 *paperback*

Typeset in Joanna
by Koinonia Limited, Manchester
Printed in Great Britain
by Bell & Bain Limited, Glasgow

Contents

Acknowledgements

I would like to thank the following:

For commissioning articles which allowed me to experiment in public with some of the material presented here, Stephen Pope and Richard Johnson.

For the joint work we did, Antonio Melechi – A 'post'-script was first published, in an earlier version, as Antonio Melechi and Steve Redhead: 'The Fall of the Acid Reign' in *New Statesman and Society*, 23/30 December 1988; thanks to Sally Townsend for editorial help.

For help with an early version of Chapter 1, Roger Ingham and the other members of the editorial board of the journal *Leisure Studies*. The article was eventually published under the title 'Don't Go Back To Rockville' in *Leisure Studies* 8, 1989.

For her consistently valuable support and constructive criticism, Ruth Redhead.

For his unstinting efforts on my behalf, John Banks.

For their initial editorial work, Jonathan Dollimore and Alan Sinfield.

For a travel grant, the Faculty of Humanities, Law and Social Science at Manchester Polytechnic.

For their time, encouragement and expertise: Steve Barker, Dave Haslam, Adrian Sherwood, Neil Duxbury, John Peel, Eugene McLaughlin, Simon Frith, John Street, Mark Aherne, Derek Wynne, Dave Horrocks, Johnny Dawe, Phil Korbel, Tim Chambers, and Joern Kroeger.

For their general assistance: Keith Le Blanc, Doug Wimbish, Skip McDonald, Bernard Fowler, Gary Clail, Alison Martin, Pete Lawrence, Dave White, Sally Reeves, Chris Cutler, WOMAD, John Empson, Sophie Bourbon, Jerry Bullivant, Dave Giles, Martin Whitehead, Pete Thompson, Charles Taylor, Gary Cope, Davyth Fear, Rhys at Anhrefn Records, Riobard Mac Gorain, Clive Gregson, Hammy at Peaceville Records, Lance Williamson, all at Southern Studios, Gorwel Owen, Grant at Ace Records, Paula Greenwood, Martin Truckle, Celluloid Records, Greensleeves Records, Coda Records, Tim at One Little Indian Records, Enzo Walther Hamilton, Barbie at StreetSounds/Westside, SST Records, Ian Scott, Colin Davies, Geoff Davies, Allan Campbell and Neil Dalgleish.

For first commissioning me to write about this subject in happier days at Pluto Press, Pete Ayrton.

For including material in their excellent Chasing Rainbows series at an early stage of the research for this book, Jeremy Marre and David Toop.

From my generation to regeneration: a 'post'-script

A handbill from Manchester's Haçienda proclaimed:

> December 21st HOT
> THE FINAL PARTY
> A CELEBRATION OF THE SUMMER OF 88

In this way, the 'Summer of Love, 88', itself a reworking of another mythical summer, took its place in the hallowed hall of pop legends. Whilst the 1960s once slipped lazily into the early 1970s, Pop Time had now accelerated with a vengeance – as if reclaiming borrowed time – according the public phenomenon of Acid House little more than a long weekend. Or, as the magazine *i-D* had it, 'three weeks and two days'. The media story was, more than ever, flash in the pan pop, truly the era of overnight sensations. An elegy began for a lost summer, because in so many ways it never really happened. A fictional summer was mourned. A lament was played for the unrealised moments, for those missed opportunities. In the times of the signs, who ever said nostalgia's not what it used to be?

The pop chroniclers of Acid House spent the Autumn of 1988, and much of 1989, investigating an allegory, unravelling its various, diverse strands. Revealing the stolen signifiers, a 'style with no substance', as the *Sunday Times* put it, was exposed, and once again the circular time scales, increasingly identified as 'postmodern', were invoked. 'If they had been born 10 years earlier they would have been punk rockers ... 20 years taken LSD and listened to Jim Morrison', suggested the *Sunday Times* on October 30, 1988. The tale was that Acid House was nothing new; it was merely another, much lauded, link in the subcultural chain, replaying and reworking the 1950s, 1960s or 1970s – the 'Golden Age' of youth culture and youth subcultures. But Acid House was not a new subculture in this sense, nor was it the long-desired 'new punk'. Previous theorists of post-war pop and deviance had tended to look beneath, or behind, the surfaces of the shimmering mediascape in order to discover the 'real' subculture, apparently always distorted by the manufactured press and television 'image'. Such explanations, however, can now finally be laid to rest. The problem for pop history is that they throw into the melting pot the accepted theories and histories of the connections between pop and deviance.

As the appropriations of Acid House were traced, a catalogue of plunderings was compiled, an enticing shopping list for the intending Acid Houser: psychedelia, Acid, smiley, beachwear, Lucozade, fluorescent paraphenelia, and so on. This was the logic of consumerism writ large. A mainly middle-class, Dionysian culture, abandoning (that is, spending) and offering itself to the market. The music in question – contrary to the *Observer*'s characterisation of it as a 'type of rock music' – fused two forms, both based on sampling . Acid House, a derivative of Chicago House music dance styles which had their origin in gay clubs, arrived in the UK around 1985. Debate still rages over which groups of people and which cities first imported house in general, and, subsequently, Acid House in particular. Whatever its specific origin it eventually came to mingle with Balearic Beat, a crazy mixture of Euro-Pop, previously exclusive to an Ibizan jet set, which pilfered from Peter Gabriel, New Order and Mandy Smith amongst others. The sound of Acid House was hailed as the acme of reconstitution.

The summer was over when on October 1, the *Sun* signalled the dawn of Acid House as 'cool and groovy'. Then, just as swiftly, the paper took an about turn and captained an offensive of 'panic' proportions indicated by headlines like: The *Sun* EVIL OF ECSTASY (October 19); The *Post* BAN THIS KILLER MUSIC (October 24); The *Sun* ACID HOUSE HORROR (October 25); The *Sun* DRUG CRAZED ACID HOUSE FANS (October 28); The *Sun* GIRL 21 DROPS DEAD AT ACID DISCO (October 31); The *Mirror* ACID KIDS LURED TO HOLLAND (November 14).

A chorus of celebrities was called to comment on the state of the nation's youth. Sir Alastair Burnet gravely presented the television crew 'evidence' of drug use at illegal warehouse parties, only to find his News At Ten broadcast inevitably sampled on a record, echoing the Renegade Sound Wave's earlier use of the programme's theme music and Big Ben chimes. Jonathan King preferred to 'call it rubeeesh'. Peter Powell, a Radio 1 disc jockey, thought it 'the closest thing to mass zombiedom'. Matt Goss, from teen stars Bros, told of his mate who had been to an Acid House club, where everybody was 'out of their heads', and 'sensible Rick' Astley astutely noted that 'they may as well call it heroin house'.

Indeed, the media account they referred to was one of 'chilling' dimensions: a tabloid version of the bogeyman, steeped in the familiar language of the horror story. Acid Pied Pipers, the 'Mister Bigs' of Acid House – unscrupulous drug dealers and warehouse party organisers – were witnessed in a seduction of the innocent. Magical bogeymen tempted their unsuspecting prey with their evil wares: Ecstasy, Acid, 'Killer Music' that cast its alluring spell. Smiley, here, became a sinister calling card with hypnotic properties, as the unfortunate were sucked into the 'hellish nightmare'.

The potential victims in this tale of an evil cult, which the tabloids recounted, promptly materialised, as the generalities of 'youths', 'teenagers' and 'schoolchildren' gave way to specifically gendered subjects. The *Sun* on November 7 told how '14 year old Jenny' swallowed Ecstasy for the first time. The *Mirror* on the same day explained the way in which a 'young girl rolled a joint of cannabis', and how 'three young girls were spotted taking the mind blowing drug LSD', and, further, quoted one 17-year-old girl claiming 'I had some Acid on me'. This portrayal of the typical Acid House victim as a young woman culminated in the *Sun* headline on November 24 of 'Acid Fiends Spike Page 3 Girl's Drink'. It was reported how Spanish men who were spiking girls' drinks 'would lie in wait and rape them'. In this case, the greater danger of sexual violation – only previously implied in the talk of sex orgies, outrageous romps and use of the 'sex drug' Ecstasy at Acid House parties – was made explicit. Women were thus established as the victims of deviance within the Acid House scene.

In the development of this media narrative, women were fast becoming the targets of a double threat, not only of the physical perils of Acid itself, but ultimately the danger of sexual abuse. As Page 3 girl Tracy Kirby reported, 'apart from the rape attempt, the worst thing was hallucinating about those ants'. Given the jeopardy that the evil of Acid House presented to women, they were, ironically, also constructed as figures of deviance within it, transgressive in a cult whose only 'legitimate' victims were male – like Gary Haisman, the disc jockey from D-Mob, who, the *Mirror* reported, found that his chart success with the single 'We Call It Acieed' rebounded on him when the tabloid papers' connection of drugs and Acid House led to cancellation of bookings all over the country.

These features of the public face of Acid House, white, male, middle-class, matched that of another media-induced figure in the allegory which became known as the 'Summer of 88'; namely, the 'lager lout'. Ministerial rhetoric, especially that of John Patten and Douglas Hurd at the Home Office, emphasised the rural dimensions of the young male with too much money to spend and too much lager inside him, who threatened formerly 'peaceful' country towns and villages – in sharp contrast to the concentration on 'young black' male inner-city rioters in earlier years of the decade. In June, the mass media focused on an Association of Chief Police Officers report that more than two thousand people were arrested in more than 250 serious public order disturbances between 1987 and 1988, mainly located in the Home Counties. The heartlands of these 'rural riots' were Thames Valley, Hampshire, Surrey and Suffolk – electorally, typically Tory strongholds. The reason for the attention given to the report in early summer was the spate of newly reported disorders in Crowborough, Newbury, Godalming, Andover and other 'rural' spots. One police Chief Inspector, John Hoyle of Dorking police, was quoted as saying that 'most of these arrested have been local people, aged between 18 and 25. They seem to have plenty of money to spend and in most cases they have been drinking ... There were flash points before. In the '60s it was mods and rockers, in cafes. Now it's in the pubs.' A Home Office Research and Planning Unit report[1] on the 'problem' of 'lager louts', presented to Parliament in the spring of 1989, identified them as young men who have not found their role in society and without the money to go on to nightclubs after the pub. The media reports stressed that many of them want instant kicks – women, fast cars, holidays and money – and proclaimed that their hero was Prince Charles because he is rich and has an attractive wife.

Conservative fears, such as those exhibited by Douglas Hurd and John Patten which were themselves regurgitations of previous statements earlier in the decade by Margaret Thatcher and Norman Tebbit, invoked the 1960s legacy of 'permissiveness' to rationalise this apparently difficult political problem of law and order. After many years of Tory rule, and the widely proclaimed phenomenon of the new Conservative and conformist youth culture culminating in the pervasive 'yuppie' spirit, the rural riots and lager louts presented a dreadful spectre of the re-emergence of deviant subcultures. For a government riding high after a third successive General Election victory this might have seemed to be a political stumbling block. Yet the apparent dilemma – for Tory Ministers – of the 'well-heeled hooligan', brought with it a scapegoat which could be turned to their own advantage. As long as the stress could be placed on 'middle-class', 'affluent' youth whose violence was caused by alcohol abuse, the conventional 'left' argument that social conditions lead to crime would be nullified. Furthermore, this justified the already accelerating return to 'law and order', elsewhere prompted by the 'new wave' of football violence at Wembley (England versus Scotland, replayed a year later in Glasgow) and Stamford Bridge (Chelsea versus Middlesbrough) in May, with the European Championships looming in June.

The Summer of Acid House marked a space in which this gallery of rogues could congregate. For instance, the *News of the World* ran a story on October 30 which had the predictable 1960s figure, notorious Acid Head Syd Barrett – a founder member of Pink Floyd – ushered in as the lead role in a classic parable of middle-class demise. This moral tale traced the fall of 'Tragic Syd' from 'Pink Floyd rock legend' to a 'pathetic, crazed zombie ... howling like a dog'. Others who auditioned for a part in this unfolding drama included 'organised gangs of football hooligans such as West Ham's ICF or Inter City Firm' who *The Illustrated London News* in its October 1988 issue linked to the Ecstasy market. Football terrace chants became ever more ingenious: Oldham Athletic fans, for instance, chorused 'Latieeecs'!

Media publicity about Acid House refocused attention on the city – but the outskirts, the margins of the urban environment, not the inner-city which Margaret Thatcher targeted as ripe for political conquest through policies of 'regeneration'. This was, manifestly, the sound of the suburbs. Warehouses, which had been extensively, and illegally, used for Acid House, and other, gatherings symbolised the problems of time and space in the so-called 'post-industrial' city. Football grounds, shopping centres, tube and railway stations were, as the 1970s merged into the 1980s, increasingly put under intense surveillance. Empty warehouses, artefacts from the industrial past (in Britain, that is *before* Thatcher) of cities such as Liverpool, Manchester, Sheffield, Bradford and Leeds, became the last refuge of hedonistic youth in search of a 'good time'. However, police raids made even these spaces vulnerable to a global, neighbourhood watch; as Chief Inspector David Hanna of Hampshire police said after one Acid House party raid, 'we would ask all responsible people to contact the police if they become aware of these parties, some of which have resulted in tragic consequences'. Amendments to Local Government and Public Order legislation in order to further tighten the policing grip on what the mass media persisted in calling Acid House parties were being urgently considered by Tory ministers as the end of the decade approached.

Of all the new signs which the 'Summer of 88' posted via the Acid House story, the 'trance dance' best registered potential shifts in the ground previously occupied by subcultures. If in contrast to punk, disco represented a re-emphasis of the 'male gaze', and more traditional notions of sexual relations, Acid House offered something of a departure. In a dance which required 'no expertise whatsoever', there was a fracturing of the conventions which have commonly structured the body in dance in pop history. Instead of, as usual, the female body being subjected to the ever-present 'look', the dancers (not just on the dancefloor but everwhere in range of the music) turned in on themselves, imploding the meanings previously associated with exhibitionist dance. In Acid House, and connected scenes, dancing no longer solely represented the erotic display of the body. Despite this, the media narrative overdosed on the sexual deviance which Acid House 'represented', missing entirely the fact that, after Aids, sexuality has come to involve hidden dangers which leave the body (though no longer safe) as the last refuge – dangers which in themselves, according to some postmodern theorists, are the aphrodisiac, the turn-on: 'panic sex' as Arthur Kroker[2] has described it to go with the panic pop of Acid House.

Inevitably, all kinds of post-(Acid)House predictions were made in the wake of the 'fall of the Acid reign'. New Beat from Belgium, Acid Jazz, Deep House and Garage were among the 'genres' nominated as contenders. But the 1990s are unlikely to see a slowing down of the accelerating speed of Pop Time which Acid House displayed, seemingly hurtling along so quickly that it must, eventually, go backwards. The media story of Acid House shows that it is not so much a case of back to the future, as forward to the past.

1

Counter-cultures: the cultural politics of pop

Pop history seems, for some writers, to have reached something of a halt. Indeed, history in general is deemed to be less predictable than it was. That most perplexing and infuriating of cultural theorists, Jean Baudrillard, proclaimed in one conference paper that 'The Year 2000 Will Not Take Place' – though in another collection the translation, more ambiguously, reads 'The Year 2000 Has Already Taken Place'! He further asserted that we would move automatically from 1989 to 2000.[1] The reason for Baudrillard's dismissal of the 1990s is that, he believes, since we have already started the 'end of the century' party, as we are, in his view, so deeply into the revival of the past mood (or mode) we might just as well miss out the last decade of the twentieth-century altogether. Certainly, contemporary musical styles and forms (music video, 'youth television') rewind pop history with the same mixture of longing and revulsion that contemporary street styles celebrate the various pasts of youth culture: and, both do so as if there really were no tomorrow.

But there is a difference between pop and rock history, and history *per se*. Firstly, there is a perceptible, but subterranean seam, which pop archaeology has uncovered, and which is present underneath the latest top 40 single or album hit. Jeremy Marre's two ambitious, pioneering Channel 4 television series, Beats of the Heart and Chasing Rainbows, have preserved for posterity a popular music history, whether it be rockabilly, 1940s dance bands, country and western, tex-mex or reggae, which is only normally visible when there is specific national or international mass media attention on such sounds as part of the continual pop merry-go-round – in Baudrillard's sense, these cultural forms have effectively 'disappeared'. Alternatively, an event like Steve Barker's On The Wire three hour Sunday afternoon local regional programme for BBC Radio Lancashire, which has run since 1984 exhibiting an exhilirating diversity of sounds every few minutes, marks an important contemporary dig into the sheer range of popular music, both 'traditional' and 'modern'.

Secondly, post-war pop music now has its own genealogy, split into specific taxonomies such as rock and roll, psychedelia, thrash, noise, garage, punk, go-go, Hi-Nrg, funk and dub which are readily available as a resource for documentary film-makers, record collectors, disc jockeys or musicians and producers armed with the latest sampling technology or just a sharp line in pastiche. The musical styles embodied in these rock and pop discourses can be revived, reworked, quoted, parodied, and plundered almost at will.

On the other hand, popular music, in all its myriad forms, is more pervasive than ever in our supposedly postmodern culture. The sounds seep out of our television sets at all times of the day or night. On our radio, apart from rare cult programmes, it substitutes for the disc jockeys when they run out of prattle. On the train or bus it leaks from turned up Walkmans. Combined with fast-flickering subliminal images, it appears to be forever selling, soothing, celebrating, hustling, commiserating and titillating. It is written and talked about, evaluated and condemned, in a series of interlocking processes. What is significant about pop is not the question of its repression, its association with deviant behaviour as such, but, following Michel Foucault's notion about the history of sexuality, the way its historical development has witnessed an increasing 'incitement to discourse'. This book is not so much a study of the forms of discourse *in* popular music as a contemporary archaelogy of discourse *on* pop. As with 'sexuality', what remains important is the forever-changing shape and contours of the field of pop music culture which becomes the subject of 'regulation', 'discipline' and 'policing'. It should be remembered, too, that popular music forms part of a leisure sphere which is ever more carefully controlled and regulated whilst it is undergoing major economic and technological transformation in the name of economic liberal policies of de-regulation, privatisation and regeneration.

In any case, it is a popular music which is no longer simply 'youth' music; music that became associated with the post-war construction of notions like the teenager, generation gap, youth culture, and youth subculture is now assisting in the imminent destruction of these categories. Heralds of the 'end of youth culture' are by implication predicting the 'death of rock culture' too. One such Nostradamus of contemporary youth styles, Toby Young,[2] even went as far as to argue, in 1985, that 'youth culture' had actually ceased to exist:

> The term 'youth culture' is at best, of historical value only, since the customs and mores associated with it have been abandoned by your actual young person ... The point is that today's teenager is no longer promiscuous, no longer takes drugs, and rarely goes to pop concerts. He leaves all that to the over-25's . . . Whatever the image adopted by teenagers now, it has to have one necessary condition: it must have nothing to do with being a teenager.[3]

However empirically inaccurate, and gender-biased, this snapshot from the confines of an Oxford college may be, the proclamation of the abandonment of 'youth culture' by the young in the 1980s needs serious consideration. Compounding Young's spurious observation, it is becoming an advertisers' cliche to see recent youth styles and consumer choices as evidence of a 'new conformism' amongst the under-25 age group as the £250 Mintel report *Youth Lifestyles* suggested in 1988. It is, however,rather less the case that a once 'rebellious' or 'deviant' youth culture has become conformist, than that the discourses and practices which constructed and positioned youth culture historically after the Second World War are now undergoing profound transformation. 'Youth television', for example, is fast becoming the new international pop style created by television and advertising discourses for the whole potential audience, irrespective of age.

Rock ideology

The idea of a 'rock culture' came back into British pop discourse in the mid-late 1980s. In the decade following punk, not only the personalities but many of the ideals and values, as well as musical forms and conventions, of 1960s and early 1970s rock resurfaced. 'New Rock'appeared as a music press and marketing category alongside familiar terms such as 'New Age', 'New Country' and 'New Authenticity', to mark out a space in popular culture for an enduring series of myths. Not that this social movement has been universally welcomed, or evenly transmitted, across the whole pop culture of the modern world. Most of the new 'white rock' in the USA and UK in the 1980s sounded, and strutted, much like the old. British and American groups in the mid-1980s, who followed in the wake of the popular success of 'blue-collar' male rockers like Bruce Springsteen and John Cougar Mellencamp, were largely 'born again' versions of their musical parents of an earlier generation. Bands such as The Long

Ryders, Guadalcanal Diary, Green on Red, Rain Parade, Jason and the Scorchers, The Weather Prophets, The Cult, for instance, frequently did little more than replicate the late 1960s and early 1970s rock aesthetic of Jefferson Airplane, Grateful Dead, Doors, Byrds, Creedence Clearwater Revival, Steppenwolf, and Buffalo Springfield.

Alongside the musical form itself came a resuscitation of rock 'meanings': what the music stood for, what, and who, it represented. The 'pop critique' of rock, which culminated in Paul Morley and Trevor Horn's hiring and eventual firing of original Merseyside 'scallies' Frankie Goes To Hollywood – subsequently provoking Holly Johnson's successful court case against ZTT -had dominated pop discourse for a decade. Politicisation of pop in Britain in the period from the mid-1970s to the mid-1980s depended, mainly, on the notion of pop as an 'art' form, rather than, as in pre-punk days, rock as a 'folk' form. Whether, as consumers of the music press mythologies have claimed, it was indeed U2, or Simple Minds, or The Smiths, or REM (or whoever) that constituted the 'last' great rock monument in pop culture remained, largely, beside the point. The influence of 'rock culture' lies beyond any simple analysis of its political economy – in other words it involves analysis of more than just its market potential, its part in patterns of profitability. Music industry corporate strategies have shifted significantly since the late 1970s, necessitating the creation and targeting of multiple new consumer categories, as well as the exploitation of rights in 'intellectual property' (copyright in songs, for instance) rather than merely the orthodox reliance on selling as many 'units' (albums, singles, compact discs, T-shirts and so on) as possible.

In this new, much changed, climate what is important is pop and rock's proven ability to produce and circulate more than just commodities. Rock and pop discourses have produced, over the last forty years, a range of individual positions (styles, poses, identities, narratives, desires) which youth culture can occupy. They have helped to create and construct youth culture as a collective subject: for addressing, marketing, cajoling, consoling and so on. It is already manifestly obvious that part of pop and rock's cultural power lies in the proven ability to create new subjects, both collective and individual, *and* new objects – to be desired, consumed, regurgitated. For some writers, moreover, it is the production and circulation of meaning that matters most in the cultural politics of pop and rock. It is primarily the messages of its own cultural force – to bind disparate populations in 'community', to be 'authentic', and 'truthful'- which rock discourse has set up as the crucial criteria for success. Its fulfilment of this regime of effectiveness has been, frequently, judged in terms of yoking successive, notionally rebellious youth subcultures (homeboys, mods, teds, skins, hippies, soulboys, ragamuffins, rastas, punks) to specific musical forms. Images of non-conformity and deviance, even criminality, have been inexorably circulated in a spectacular testament to rock's durable effect. Punk is the best example. Subculture, style and sound shrink-wrapped for the pop culture archive. It represents not the end of the pop/rock/youth culture nexus but its most perfect product.

Punk ideology certainly did manage, fleetingly, to discredit the rock myths which were manifestly decaying by the mid-1970s. It did so by laying bare the business techniques and tactics involved in its own production. Punk exposed, albeit for a very short time, the continuance of capital's role in the pop process by (two) fingering the moneymakers, who were more often than not the same entrepreneurs as in pre-punk days. One of the many, contradictory, effects of punk was that it better prepared subsequent New Pop (in the limited sense of Duran Duran, Wham!, Spandau Ballet, Culture Club) stars for the task of attempting to control their own destinies to a greater degree than ever before. They had ample notice of the 'scam' dominated record industry through Julian Temple and Malcolm McLaren's film *The Great Rock and Roll Swindle*' by the time their own careers started to take off in the early 1980s. Consequently, they were often able to employ self-conscious business practices more easily whilst still playing the traditional role of pop star for all it was worth. On the other hand, as has been very well documented, there was ruthless exploitation of even these more canny performers' slightest naivety over music industry contracts. Despite the 1980s incarnation of the 'pop star as businessman', what was clear was that rock ideology, as with previous pop upheavals, was far from extinguished.

By 1984, conference participants in Australia, meeting to consider 'Excursions into Post-Modernity', could lament the passing of, as they saw it, the style and irony of certain post-punk, or New Pop, heroes (for instance, ABC, Human League, and Scritti Politti) whilst registering their profound disapproval of the 'return' to rock values:

> In the Eighties, the heavy referentials of rock ideology . . . are making a big comeback - power, stature, direct speech, the authenticity of energy . . . Even if the sound of rock hasn't completely swamped us in the wake of its return

– and even if record producers can still smuggle into the studio, unseen in the rock video, the drum machine and the sequencer – still its rhetoric, its catalogue of poses and gestures, threatens to. Take the essential notions, in rock ideology, of presence, live performance and direct speech, 'speakin at ya' in some apparently raw and immediate state.[4]

Rock, as a cultural description and an ideology of specific content, for these writers at least, was a reactionary incursion into a far more seductive 'pop' culture. Theirs was a self-confessed 'post-punk' rather than a punk critique, emanating from an 'ethos of mid-to-late 70's New Wave ... of sophisticated irony, of the proudly and cagily synthetic and plastic'.[5] Whatever we may make of their own nostalgic musings on an era so recently buried, they correctly identified, as early as 1984, what were becoming the 'new modalities for gestures of spontaneity and authenticity' as rock oriented. They made clear too, that these characteristics ranged right across the breadth of popular music in the 1980s to include rap, soul, African, roots and the folk'n'roll of the ubiquitous Bruce Springsteen.

The cultural politics of pop today depend on an accurate assessment of these conditions and contexts. What is intriguing is that attempts to politicise pop have, increasingly, been based around the terms of rock ideology, and the extent of the successes and failures of a new formation in popular culture that might be called Political Pop (exemplified by, for instance, performers as different as Youssou N'Dour, Little Steven, UB 40, The Style Council, The Redskins, Easterhouse, Billy Bragg, The Housemartins, and The Communards) can only be estimated once their traces have been identified. This new cartography of pop tastes may also hasten understanding of the complex legacy of New Pop, and what became of its post-punk ancestry. It is this pop 'moment', a new re-combination of 'synthetic/authentic' terms, which now forms the significant historical reference point for understanding the contorted relations of pop, rock and deviance rather than the more distant outrages of punk.

Political pop

Popular music today, at first sight, seems a strange, even bizarre, focus for notions of political resistance and deviance. Pop-saturated adverts, the selling of the Beastie Boys and other hyper-commercialised pop,

Sigue Sigue Sputnik's deliberately trivial re-run of the Sex Pistols story for the twenty-first century, the 'whitening' of Michael Jackson, and the global imperialism of the giant companies in the various culture and leisure industries, suggest an overwhelming conformity to political and economic conservatism. Prince's often brilliantly outrageous re-articulation of pop myths from Jimi Hendrix to Little Richard is still predicated on a religious conformism and traditional portrayal of women as sex objects, despite his refreshing re-examination of 'masculinities' in pop identity. Racism, sexism, masculine aggression and greedy self-aggrandisement pervade pop values and practices, just as they dominate other spheres. However, as a site of intersecting cultural struggles, pop has, once again, become a vital arena. One persuasive, conventional notion of pop's power has been gathering strength during the decade, perceiving in the 'folk' cultural expression of rock music an opposition to the (according to this version) cynical, exploitative, shallow and thoroughly commodified, commercialised pop culture underlying it. The 'counter-culture' of the 1960s relied, in part, on this sort of rock critique; so, too, did some readings of the significance of punk. As in earlier versions of sub-cultural or youth cultural music in the mid-late 1960s and early 1970s, there was seen to be a folk ideology at work. As Simon Frith has argued, though, 'rock operates as counter-culture only at moments'.[6] Similar claims to those made for the 'hippy' moment of the 1960s and the 'punk' moment of the 1970s, were reiterated in the 1980s. What this argument comes up against is the insistence that pop succeeds (politically, emotionally, socially) by drawing on other resources: for instance, its role as an 'art' form. As Frith has put it in relation to the 1960s and 1970s:

> It was explicitly to explore the hard edges of youthful frustration that punk emerged a decade later, but its commercial development, too, seemed to confirm the argument that rock can express the values of specific communities only briefly. Rock, in other words, is rarely a folk music ; its cultural work is done according to different rules.[7]

The view that musical forms can express community of any kind is indeed fraught with difficulty. There is, initially, the objection that the community itself is constructed, to some extent, through the medium of the musical form, and not the other way round. 'New Country'-oriented singers like The Judds, Dwight Yoakam, Nanci Griffith, Lyle Lovett, Randy Travis, and Steve Earle cannot simply be seen as reflecting a pre-constituted set of American 'country' values.

Folk ideology, or the idea that a musician/performer directly represents a constituency (nation, locality, subculture), also has to confront the problem of 'legitimacy', or the 'right' to speak or sing out on behalf of a community. The Pogues' ambiguous relationship to the Irish community in Britain is an interesting illustration, given some band members' public school background and frequent 'drunken Irish' stereotyping in their media coverage. Different, but related difficulties, face an avowedly Irish 'Republican' pop band like That Petrol Emotion. But even more testing is the question of the pre-existence of 'given' communities at all. There is the argument, for example, that we 'are all members of numerous collectivities, numerous communities, which often hold contradictory beliefs and attitudes'.[8] Pop and rock music's association with nationalism and regionalism becomes ever more crucial for the question of how pop can be politicised, as the internationalisation – even globalisation – of pop music culture continues apace. An independent label such as Cooking Vinyl can self-consciously dedicate itself to 'neither London nor Los Angeles' but as 'internationalist', whilst still being economically dependent on the commercial pop success of 'world' and 'roots' music. Probe Plus, a label with a manic variety of artists from the hardcore of Walking Seeds to the pop of Jegsy Dodd and the Sons of Harry Cross, is faced with prejudices about how 'authentic' Liverpool bands should sound, generated by Mersey beat myths perpetuated since the early 1960s, involving such diverse pop traditions as the Beatles, Echo and the Bunnymen and the Christians. The same problem occurs at a national level: how far can, for instance, Hue and Cry, the Proclaimers, Fairground Attraction and Deacon Blue be taken to 'represent' a distictively Scottish music, or The Triffids, Midnight Oil and The Go-Betweens signify an Australian music?

It has been widely suggested that a move back to 'authenticity' after the self-conscious 'play' of the New Pop era was identifiable as *the* pop moment of the mid-late 1980s. A variety of musical forms were 'rediscovered', during this period, in the compulsive search for 'roots' – among them folk, reggae, country, psychedelia, soul, gospel, rockabilly and whole varieties of 1950s, 1960s, 1970s pop. These forms reappear, however, throughout pop's family tree, in different guises and combinations. As always, their meanings in any one context are mediated through the multiple consumer guides of the age: from the tabloid press pop pages to *Smash Hits*, *i-D* and *Blitz*, through *New Musical Express* and *Melody Maker* to *Rolling Stone* and *Q*, and the hundreds of specialist and regional fanzines and listings magazines, to multifarious TV and radio offerings. Issues relating to the politics of 'authenticity/syntheticity' cannot be analysed without recourse to this contemporary explosion of discourse on/in pop and rock. Fresh pop styles, images and meanings are produced in this mass of interlocking and contradictory texts.

One of the most obvious fashions to enter the pop market-place in the 1980s was, somewhat ironically, protest. New Popsters galore queued up to jump aboard the social conscience bandwagon set rolling by Bob Geldof and Midge Ure's Band Aid venture. For instance, Gary Kemp of Spandau Ballet played acoustic guitar at concerts organised by Red Wedge, a collective of musicians and other artists set up to promote Labour Party policies, which also produced its own quarterly journal, *Well Red* to further inform and update the redefinition of pop protest, rebellion and revolt. Wham! performed at a benefit for the British miners' strike of 1984-5, and U2 and Simple Minds played for Amnesty International. Individual personal conviction, what might be referred to as 'putting your mouth where your money is', became an important pop mode in the later part of the decade, as more and more benefit causes (Aids, the banning of the promotion of homosexuality by the Local Government Act 1988, heroin abuse, 'green' campaigns or, more mundanely, the saving of a local pop venue) have multiplied. The depth of the performer's loyalty to the particular issue, though, was less at stake than the shift which was taking place in pop sensitivity.

The conventional musical form of protest, namely guitar, vocal, concerned lyrics, itself experienced something of a boom in popularity, deriving sustenance from troubadours and singer/songwriters who shook off their early 1970s image and connotations, allowing performers as socially and politically diverse as Paddy McAloon (of Prefab Sprout), Roddy Frame (of Aztec Camera), Lloyd Cole (and the Commotions), Tracy Chapman, and Suzanne Vega to reap the unexpected benefits of a substantial listening and viewing public. After what were seen as boys' toys had tended to dominate New Pop (one young man and his synthesiser), Political Pop created a space on record company agendas for 'serious' female solo artists like Enya, Tanita Tikaram, and Gail Ann Dorsey, in stark contrast to the young 'wannabees' who followed in the footsteps of Madonna such as Debbie Gibson and Tiffany. In 1987, BBC Radio 1 disc jockey John Peel hosted a broadcast documentary history entitled Rebel Yell, which emphasised the solid traditions of protest, rooted in folk sensibilities. But a much wider notion of protest, derived from folk ideology rather than simply folk music, came to the fore. A whole swathe of musical forms from varieties of hardcore (for instance, bands like Sonic Youth, Big Dipper, Dead Kennedys, Black Flag, Big Black, Butthole Surfers) to 'folk/country punk' (such as Nick Cave and the Bad Seeds, We Free Kings, Gone To Earth, Eugene Chadbourne, Camper Van Beethoven) were touted for their continuation of pop's link with nonconformity, dissent and social deviance, though embodying widely differing notions of protest in the process. Furthermore, various regional African musics, as well as soca, calypso and hip-hop, proved just as capable of being understood in folk protest terms as Appalachian or Celtic music.

There is no intrinsic reason why, for instance, the electro-pop 1970s bands like Kraftwerk or 1980s versions like New Order or the Pet Shop Boys should not be as successful pop protest as one man, or woman, and their guitar. Further, the instrument frequently in question of most significance is the voice. The venomous social comment of Elvis Costello, for instance, is integrally related to the way he slurs what he says, a style developed in manufacturing all of his brilliant, ephemeral pop bubblegum. He managed to construct a model form of pop protest in the Thatcher years: resentful, bitter, damaged. 'Peace in Our Time', and even 'Shipbuilding', recorded at the time of the Falklands war so evocatively by Robert Wyatt, displayed the facets of conventional protest songs – however obliquely – in lyric, style and instrumentation. But 'Tokyo Storm Warning' (deliberately echoing the Rolling Stones 'Nineteenth Nervous Breakdown' from the late 1960s) and 'I Want You', released as singles from the *Blood and Chocolate* album recorded with the Attractions in 1986, brought out the devoted and the devastated in his pop persona. They remain chilling in their political and personal desolation. 'Tramp the Dirt Down' from the 1989 LP *Spike – The Beloved Entertainer* reached a pinnacle in such a musical form marrying lilting Irish traditional music and brutal lyrics aimed at Margaret Thatcher's social and political responsibility for her decade in power.

However, the very diversity of such musical styles currently proliferating should not be taken as an expression of, or in some way a testament to, a new 'counter-culture' which had gradually emerged in the post-punk years. It would be a mistake to see in such formations a straightforward rebirth of the idea of a 1960s music-based oppositional force. As has been observed elsewhere,[9] it is debilitating to revive counter-cultural criteria, as if it was possible to politicise pop by operating outside or beyond pop and rock discourse in the late twentieth-century global village. Such application of rock theory inevitably leads to a disarming cultural and political pessimism because such criteria no longer apply; indeed, they were always misleading. Where they are still employed there is a danger of obscuring what might be yet important about 'protest' or 'socially conscious' pop, or, more significantly, Political Pop as a new cultural formation: what may make concerts on behalf of Amnesty, Live Aid, Farm Aid, Comic Relief, Self Aid, and Artists Against Apartheid worthy of more than either fatalistic despair or reluctant approval.[10] The problem is not one, as rock theory has consistently argued, of 'incorporation' of counter-cultural rock ideologies and practices into those of the glossy, advertising world of 'pop culture': it is not a straightfoward question of 'selling out', or of faded idealism.The prophets of the new pluralism, those who uncritically welcome the healthy diversity of a pop musical postmodernism – 'anything goes' – tend to forget that pop's reputation for being the commodity most famous for selling itself has been built on precisely such a range of consumer tastes all through the post-war period. For example, Manchester tape label Bop Cassettes boasts a phenomenal variety of global music from Northern soul through Asian folk, to hip-hop, soul and funk, but however laudable such an enterprise, the various sounds themselves are not innately oppositional. Resistance in popular music discourses needs to be theorised differently if sense is to be made of the rapid, and disorientating, changes occurring in the leisure and culture fields. There is one possibility, for example, as Michel Foucault suggested, of theorising power as producing multiple resistances.[11] 'Counter-cultures' in pop and rock music discourses are in no way separate from, or outside such authority. They are, rather, directly produced by such discourses. Counter-cultures, as it is used in this book, is a phrase pregnant with double meaning. Its use here has at least as much to do with shopping and consumption as with opposition and the 1960s counter-culture. The pun on shop counter is resonant of many political and economic debates about the mid-late 1980s consumer booms, especially in the United Kingdom, engineered as they were by a kind of 'electoral Keynesianism'[12] on the part of the British Tory government. However, other pioneering attempts to develop analyses along these lines have floundered, to some extent on the uncritical retention of the concepts of youth culture and counter-culture to explain the working of pop as we approach the millenium.

In some ways, for many cultural critics, the later years of the century are beginning to symbolise a long predicted political nightmare, manifesting its repressive and authoritarian effects on the cultural sphere in particular. In the 1980s, the spectre of poverty and unemployment, camouflaged by massaged government statistics and youth training schemes, amounted to Britain's version of the Enlightenment dream turning in upon itself. Rapidly disintegrating and dilapidated public services sat alongside shiny, bright new private provision and burgeoning areas of individual affluence, guaranteeing entrenched electoral majorities for politicians of the 'new' or 'radical' right. A rabidly voracious music industry still gorged itself on the last of the big spenders, the post-war 'baby boomers'. Circulation-crazed newspapers threw up any old story that flung together pop, lust and addiction; the new version of sex, drugs and rock'n'roll as a particularly nasty tale. Those interests and authorities dedicated to the censorship,and prohibitive moral regulation, of pop and rock music culture (prefigured in the USA by the Parents Music Resource Centre – the PMRC) specifically singled out genres such as noise, hardcore punk and speed metal for special attention. This created the kind of media moral panic which led to the ultimately unsuccessful American court action against Jello Biafra, former leader of the Dead Kennedys, and the police surveillance and criminal prosecutions of independent record shops and distributors (such as Manchester's Eastern Bloc, amongst others) for selling records such as the double LP by Flux of Pink Indians entitled *The Fucking Cunts Treat Us Like Pricks* and released on the One Little Indian label -a case where the record company involved also explicitly campaigned for funds to be sent to the No Censorship campaign which helped finance the legal defence of the Dead Kennedys as well as Flux.

However, this is a relatively conventional view of pop and deviance, steeped in rock theory produced in the 1960s and 1970s. It suggests that power is something which is exercised by the state against a deviant object – in this case popular music. The (rock) community which such music is deemed to represent can then be mobilised in a politics of resistance, organised around historical notions of deviant identities: a youth or counter culture – a new bohemia. This rock critique is disabled, though, when for once in the trajectory of popular music since the Second World War, the middle of a decade has not seemed to produce a political, social or cultural upheaval. The middle years of the 1950s, 1960s and 1970s all reputedly witnessed spectacles (labelled variously as rock 'n'roll, the 'British pop invasion', counter-culture, punk) which led pop culture's soothsayers to predict new eruptions between the Election years – in the United States of America and the United Kingdom – of 1983-4 and 1987-8. That they were now not seen to have occurred, or rather that they were not evident in these particular cultural sites, depends to an extent on the dominant readings of what pop moments in previous decades mattered, and why. This kind of reasoning – evidenced in all the extensive literature on and of rock theory – which has become embedded in pop's historical texts is part and parcel of the debates about how far house, rap and hip-hop constitute just such a moment. It may be, though, that the contemporary transitions in the discourses and practices which have so far sustained rock and youth culture are such that, in future, to produce equivalent cultural formations at all will require an altogether different cultural politics; not, however, as some have suggested, a politics of youth culture, or rock culture. Elements evident in Political Pop as a social formation, depend on a re-introduction and revising of folk and rock ideologies into popular music discourses. These ideologies, as we have already noted, are likely to be as much a liability as an advantage. Such a formation, nevertheless, can be seen to produce as its opposite the multiple sites of resistance of what might be termed Post-Political Pop: for instance, the musical cut-ups of Mark Stewart and the Maffia, Tackhead, Barmy Army, African Head Charge and Dub Syndicate – all produced by Adrian Sherwood, owner of On-U Sound Records; the distinctive house mixes of producers like Todd Terry or Marshall Jefferson; the Northern 'folk' of The Mekons, King of the Slums or The Fall; or the 'home-made' technological rhythms of 808 State and A Guy Called Gerald. The analysis and description of rock and pop music 'counter-cultures' in the 1980s which forms the basis of this book is significant for what it reveals, more generally, about the problems and possibilities of 'policing' the social field of pop music culture in the radically changed, and considerably more difficult, conditions which now pertain in the present, and which are likely to intensify in the late 1990s, and Baudrillard permitting, the year 2000.

The death of rock culture

'Rock culture' denotes a social formation which emerged after 1945 and remains a powerful source of knowledge, meaning and identity in the whole of what increasingly cultural critics label as 'postmodern culture'. However, as has been rightly pointed out, the 'historical moment of postmodernism is also the moment of the birth of rock culture'.[13]Moreover, some have gone as far as to argue that, by the later 1980s, it was clear that the 'rock era is over'.[14] Attempts to connect postmodernism as the dominant cultural logic of late capitalism as Fredric Jameson has done[15] or even, less deterministically, as the art of the next epoch[16] tend to miss this specific periodisation of the postmodern. In a sense, pop has *always* been postmodern in that it has predicated itself on the dissolution of the 'high culture/low culture' division. It has, as much as any other aesthetic practice, constantly displayed an obsession with allegory, pastiche, parody, quotation and the theft or 'piracy' of debris from previous cultural forms. What requires to be more specifically mapped are the conditions of existence of pop and rock culture: how their genesis was made historically possible, and what distinguishes one phase of pop's encounter with postmodern themes (say, the mid-late 1960s, or mid-late 1970s) from another (for example, the mid-late 1980s); what differences there are in the notion of 'avant-garde' pop from the 1960s (for example, Soft Machine), the 1970s (for instance, Henry Cow) and the 1980s (say, Test Department and Einstürzende Neubauten). The focus of this book can be seen as one, unmapped fragment of this history.

In the forty-year period since the birth of rock culture, there has been a whole series of mythologies created around the long historical transition of the story of the institution of popular music, from, at least, the nineteenth-century to the present. This narrative has involved numerous twists and turns, premature obituaries, false endings, and unfulfilled promises. One unintended consequence of such mythologies is that rock itself is now deemed to have 'roots', located in various, different 1960s (or even 1950s) memories, images, sounds and artefacts. The 1970s, in such an account of pop history, become, variously, designated as either a barren period of disillusionment, or else an era of experiment and possibility. Rock's late 1960s myths, amalgamating counter-culture with a certain mélange of musical styles (fossilising them politically in the process), have provided the raw material for a host of young bands and performers to reference pop (and youth culture) pasts even though they were not personally present in the making of such popular memory. They also sustain older musicians and singers who first built their styles and reputations in those years and could not realistically have expected a prosperous, life-long career in an industry which had institutionalised the notion of 'permanent teenage'.

Recycling the 1970s for the compact disc 1980s frequently demanded a rather partisan reconstruction of the pop signs of that decade: this view tends to play down glam-rock's androgyny and punk's garage and pub rock roots. There is, though, always ample scope for re-writing the narrative for different audiences at different times to meet various consumer markets. The sight of a cluster of ageing rock stars rattling their jewellery for royalty on Prince's Trust concert stages and records (not to mention the Prince and Princess of Wales reciprocating by tapping their feet and clapping their hands) not only recalls The Beatles' moral dilemmas in the 1960s, but emphasises the historical developmentof the formularisation of rock as 'rebellion', and underscores the respectable face of rock and pop which has constantly been present. The sheer healthiness of the popular music industry was what stood out for the casual pop consumer in the mid-late 1980s, just as it did in the mid-1970s prior to punk's emergence in 1976-7. In the shop window were the familiar selling points: the quality of digital production, the vitality of the speed and energetic movement on stage or video, and the super-efficiency of much of the playing, however simulated. These are, however, values for money, a consumer paradise where uncertainty about what needs the commodity purchased will satisfy is banished, and doubt and anxiety about the (cash or credit) transaction have no place. Spend spend spend is, here, the only pop religion.

One reason for the continuing use of rock theory to explain the evolution of the pop industry and the market success of AOR (Adult Orientated Rock) thinking is simply age. Rock is ageing and maturing with its audience. The massive future potential of rock's global audience is not only in new markets in near-virginal pop territory (China, the Soviet Union, the Eastern bloc, Africa) but in the obvious hold over its original generation which is getting older and, like pre-rock generations, sinking into political complacency born of material affluence the further away it drifts from its 'youthful' past. The career of an ageing rock star such as Eric Clapton is an interesting illustration of the performers' guide to this process. Looking back from the 'rock dinosaur' award at the British Phonographic Industry extravaganza in 1987, 'Slowhand' (no irony in the nickname any more) surveyed a quarter of a century in showbusiness.The journey from blues junkie to guitar deity in a few short years in the 1960s, followed by well-publicised heroin addiction and cure – not to mention Powellite rhetoric which helped to fuel Rock Against Racism's fire in the 1970s – turned out to be only a prelude. Pop media rehabilitation snared him comprehensively in the 1980s. Melvyn Bragg's subsequent South Bank Show tribute to him reworked this narrative for the benefit of an art media audience, flattening the peaks and troughs of Clapton's pop autobiography in the style of a television programme like the Rock'n'Roll Years, which mixed 'retro' music with newsreel flashes. Clapton himself has been quoted in the music press as saying that 'artists' inevitably lose something that motivates them at the age of around twenty-five. The more convincing explanation is that when the popular press mercilessly hunted down Boy George's drug use, or Clapton's fellow Prince's Trust co-star Elton John for his sexual preferences,[17] the moral crusade became so all-encompassing that to be so uncontroversial (and yet still widely revered by consumers, critics and record company executives alike) comes as something of a relief: a lifestyle to go with the bland-out of the music.

But the ages of rock and pop are not merely biological or psychological categories. If pop and rock can construct so effectively and pervasively, in conjunction with other mass media advertising forms, a 'youth' market over four decades, it can predictably be relied upon to sustain an 'adult' constituency. The economic and technological changes are already well advanced. There is, firstly, the prolonged long-term decline of the single, boosted by punk and 'new wave' in the 1970s, though sure to be swiftly brought to its conclusion as high street stores step up plans to stock only those discs which figure in the charts. Secondly, to connect with specific marketing to the, mainly male, over-25 audience, there is the high-speed development of new technologies such as CDs, digital audio tape cassettes (DAT), and video cassette recorders. The conflicts of production and distribution interests which may be imminent are to an extent foreshadowed in manufacture and sale of the earlier tape to tape cassette recorders which were the subject of legal action in the CBS Songs' unsuccessful civil case[18]against Amstrad in 1988. These are all highly significant 'post-punk' moves spurred, initially, by the economic crisis of the popular music industry in the late 1970s and early 1980s. Rock and pop culture's role in these shifts is certainly changing, but its effectivity is still conditional on its capacity to work on the desire to feel young.

The end of youth culture

That rock and youth culture have been so inextricably intertwined since their birth is not necessarily because there is always a connection in practice between particular youth subcultural styles and specific forms of music. Skinheads and ska in the late 1960s, rastas and reggae in the 1970s, and skateboarders and hardcore in the 1980s are instances of such 'homologies' but the links between them cannot in fact be so readily unified, nor easily predicted.What has become commonplace is the notion that the 'end' of youth culture must somehow precipitate the conclusion of the 'rock era', and vice versa. However, the very idea of the existence of such a terminal condition when applied to musical forms and life-styles contains its own difficulties. As Jean Baudrillard has commented more generally:

> I don't know if it's a question of an 'end'. The word is probably meaningless in any case, because we're no longer so sure that there is such a thing as linearity ... History has stopped meaning, referring to anything – whether you call it social space or the real. We have passed into a kind of hyper-real where things are being replayed *ad infinitum.*[19]

There has been a pronounced tendency in both 'academic' and 'popular' histories of youth culture to promote a concept of linear time. Subcultural styles are seen as unfolding, generationally, from the teds to the casuals or from punk to the present, depending on the particular focus. Youth subcultures and counter-cultures appear as having succeeded each other over a forty-year period since 1945 in a mainly masculine parade of spectacle and outrage. Beginning, initially, with the teddy boy style in the mid-1950s, working class subcultures are retrospectively mapped back on to British cultural history every few years. The mods, seen to spring from a more semi-skilled and white-collar social base than the teds, explode on to the youth cultural landscape to clash, metaphorically and literally, with unskilled rockers. Greasers, bikers and other variants emerge, though with nothing like the legendary menace of American Hell's Angels. Skinheads, metamorphosed 'hard' mods, are spotted 'taking·ends' at football grounds in the season after England's World Cup victory in 1966, before they splintered, eventually, into crombies, suedeheads and other groupings by the early 1970s. Most misleadingly of all, in this historical lineage, punks were held to be the natural inheritorsof what had become by the mid-1970s, a 'dole-queue' ethos as, particularly, youth unemployment in Britain and other Western countries started to climb. The casuals, emphasising smart, expensive clothes from either sportswear or menswear, took their place in this youth culture museum from a complex of mod, 'Bowie boys' and skinhead styles, in the 1977-8 British soccer season, though their position was only belatedly secured by a series of misguided interpretations on the part of a largely bemused mass media in the 1980s.[20]

These youth subcultural fashions were read as white styles; some urban black styles, rudies, rastas, B-boys did however receive a similar kind of treatment in youth culture histories on a parallel time scale. More middle-class styles, notably the jazz-oriented beats of the 1950s and counter-cultural hippies of the 1960s (recruited, substantially, from more upwardly mobile mods), were fitted in on the same plane. Subsequent revivals, for instance, of teds, mods, skins, hippies, and greasers, failed to disrupt the impression that what stood out in this evolution of post-war youth styles was continuity rather than circularity.The absence of women in these histories – still the most obvious gap in rock theory about pop as a whole – started to be repaired from the mid-1970s, both in terms of previous subcultural histories which could be revised to include their presence, and of a more careful observation of their role in punk, new romantic, goth and casual subcultures. Ample demonstration that the teds were not the necessary 'starting'point was provided by the spectre of the resurrected 1940s styles of the spiv and 'zoot-suiters', not to mention 1920s jazz age flappers or late nineteenth-century 'hooligan' styles.

The association of such youth groups with particular musical styles, which were also theorised as evolving in a linear fashion after the Second World War, tended to become a taken-for-granted assumption. However, subsequent analyses by Dick Hebdige, and by Iain Chambers, have begun to question the earlier orthodoxies of this brand of Cultural Studies. Importantly, there is recognition that a new era of, as Chambers puts it, 'post-subcultural styles', may have been upon us for some while, at least since punk. Yet, in fact, since the 1940s, Pop Time has, in many ways, been circular rather than linear:

the speed of what comes round again may change but the cyclical motion is embedded in pop's genealogy.

What, in practice, we witnessed in the 1980s was the break-up not simply of former theoretical traditions (or master and meta-narratives) about the emancipatory potential of youth in the West, but the disintegration and restructuring of those formations (rock culture, youth culture) which were produced as their object. 'Authentic' subcultures were produced by subcultural theories, not the other way around. In fact, popular music and 'deviant' youth styles never fitted together as harmoniously as some subcultural theory proclaimed. For instance, although rock 'n'roll in Britain came to signify delinquency by connoting the emergence of the teds in the 1950s, there was no simple historical synchronicity. As Charlie Gillett says in his classic history of pop and rock:

> Delinquency had been a growing problem before the appearance of rock 'n'roll as youths throughout the country grew increasingly dissatisfied with for one thing the facilities for entertainment and expression available to them. Dance halls played 'strict tempo' ballroom dancing music, and youth clubs tended to be run by religious groups, or watched under close supervision. Their usual clientele was sedate and orderly. But rock'n'roll brought sounds to the dance halls and youth clubs that attracted from the streets the people who had been breaking shop windows and telephone boxes and prowling round in gangs on the lookout for other gangs (and occasionally beating up old people). Sometimes the gangs reassembled at the end of the dances, or made menacing groups in cafes, which seemed to point to rock'n'roll as an evil inspiration for hoodlums. Such was the kind of evidence on which the association was based.[21]

A broadly similar comment could be formulated for all post-war youth styles and their perceived connections to pop and rock music; Acid House and hip-hop just as much as mods and rockers. The causal link between them is more often a brief, casual encounter on the highly complex and contradictory terrain of pop genealogy. The formation marked out by the term Political Pop is less a folk expression of youth subcultural angst than a register of the shift in the place of youth culture within the pop process. The association of the thefts of Volkswagen car badges with fans of the Beastie Boys may have suggested a new generation of 'bricoleurs' to follow the teds' adoption of the formerly respectable Edwardian suit, or the casuals' persistent ripping out (of context, and shops) of designer labels, but the band's mix of hip-hop and heavy metal music was of more lasting consequence. The myths of youth culture were all but exhausted by the late 1980s; the myths of popular music, on the other hand, have barely begun to be excavated. As Simon Frith has argued, '"Youth" is now just a marketing device and advertiser's fiction; the myths that matter have different sources: American funk and hip hop, the archives of psychedelia and folk-rock.'[22]

It is the recycling and re-combination of the meanings of certain pop and rock (and miscellaneous other musical, and non-musical) sounds, formats, riffs, drum patterns, networks of notes and vocal ranges that need to be described and accounted for in the cultural politics of pop music. It is this direction which needs pursuing vigorously, rather than the continued analysis of the alleged importance of the appropriation of subcultural objects (punks' bondage gear and safety pins, or goths' restaging of the *Rocky Horror Show* for instance) to communicate fresh cultural meanings. In that sense, Political and Post-Political[23] Pop may demand the disconnection of the couplet 'youth culture' and 'rock culture' for their significance to be properly appreciated.

2

It all comes round again? post-subcultural pop

The pop moment following on from that of New Pop can be described as Political Pop for a number of reasons. Its complex character is displayed in the increasing use of the pop medium, and media, to promote causes from struggles against Third World poverty or torture and imprisonment to preserving the environment – whilst simultaneously having to deny their 'political' nature (especially to accommodate financial sponsors – Pepsi executives sat in judgement on the Mandela Birthday concert at Wembley for instance) in a period of a considerable rightward surge in the general political climate and concomitant increase in the hard line pursuance of economic liberalism. However, traditional notions of left and right, or centre, political ideologies have been confounded in the way that 'pop'n'politics' mix together in this formation. The new laissez-faire, or 'enterprise culture' espoused by the radical right is, superficially, pervasive in contemporary pop, from the celebration in song of material success, and the enterprise and renewed initiative of small and medium-sized businesses recording, manufacturing, designing and distributing the various pop commodities. Organisation of Acid House, and other warehouse, parties is a case in point with sometimes thousands of people being directed to various locations up and down the country by means of car phones and other 'yuppie' paraphernalia. But the energy and verve of small, independent record labels and highly motivated individuals has been a major creative force in the international popular music industry throughout its history. Support for one or other political party, or philosophy, is not necessarily implied by such economic activity. Moreover, pop has always, in any case, been a cultural form which lent itself more to an exploration of a specifically sexual politics; it is in its relations to sexuality and gender that the politically deviant character of pop has been most pronounced since the 1940s. Further, to label this particular formation Political Pop is not to deny the politicisation of pop (post-punk, in particular, is still seen as a golden age for political pop) in earlier eras, or to suggest an improvement in its prospects, but more to register the difference in the combination of 'artifices' and 'authenticities' involved – of pop as art form and folk form.

For many commentators 'style' became a code word for the 1980s: loosely, this has been seen as a triumph of 'form' over 'content', an emphasis on packaging and look, rather than substance and sound. More specifically in pop music culture it has been used to designate a moment of dominance, of cultural hegemony, by magazines such as (the short-lived) *New Sounds, New Styles*, *The Face*, *i-D* or *Blitz*, as well as graphic designers like Neville Brody: the 'style-ographers', as they have been called[1]. More widely it has come to signify a plurality of youth, or street, *styles* which in the 1970s were theorised as embodying a displaced, or symbolic, resistance to economic and cultural change in the post-war class structure in Britain. Increasingly, though, the tendency has been to establish a new orthodoxy decrying such earlier analyses and to evaluate the meaning of such street styles along more conventional lines, emasculating the political critique given in work by writers on subcultures and race.

The New Pop fits into the frame of what has been called Style Culture in various ways. New Pop itself has evolved as a term designating cultural struggle, and hence difficult to define clearly. Paul Morley, New Pop's most prominent theorist and self-publicist, coined it in tribute to 'ABC and The Fire Engines rather than Howard Jones and Duran Duran',[2] though it has more often been used in the latter sense. What is certainly plain is that in the periods of successful penetration of their respective markets, New Pop and Style Culture have to a large extent coincided, and been mutually supportive. In both cases, the highpoints of influence were already gone by the time media saturation point arrived: these were early 1980s movements, rather than significant features of the mid-late 1980s, despite their apparent absorption into more mainstream media projects and their widespread presence in the high street. However, their repercussions on the formations of Political Pop, and Post-Political Pop, are extremely important.

The ends of Style Culture

Both subcultural studies of deviant and delinquent youth generated within the liberal theory of the 'old' American Sociological Positivist school of the 1950s and early 1960s, and the more recent Cultural Studies perspective largely associated with the work of the Centre for Contemporary Cultural Studies at the University of Birmingham had become riven with contradictions by the early 1980s. Despite their contrasting claims about American and British youth culture histories, and the extent of the material resistances to dominant cultures such groupings were seen to embody, what united them was a commitment to the 'authenticity' of youth subcultures. So, in the British case, for Cultural Studies, the teds could be portrayed (misleadingly, as we have noted) as the first 'folk devils' of the post-war period. They could also be seen as a substantially self-generating subculture, responding in a specific way to the contradictions of the 'age of affluence' as viewed from the standpoint of a certain section of lower working class British male white youth at the beginning of the 1950s. Mods, rockers, skinheads, hippies and rastas were subjected to similar theoretical criteria in analysis of the sort of distinctive youth styles which have been the object of such fascination and desire in the post-punk era. By the 1970s there was a pronounced tendency towards theoretical acknowledgement of the 'manufacture' of such styles. Glamrock, for example, was read as an instance of this counter-trend and as a definite portent of things to come.[3] Punk, though, appeared at first sight, to be more in line with a certain 'authenticity' rather than 'manufacture'; in other words, taking punk ideology at face value, it was taken as more a 'folk' expression of the street than commercial exploitation. This misreading of punk, and by implication the wholesale romanticisation of the origins of previous youth styles, led to a whole new mythology in the writing of youth culture histories and biographies which has persisted into the present. As was noted in Chapter 1, what is now being hailed is the 'death of youth culture' rather than its perennial continuation in a straight line of historical time, but it is based on the notion that such subcultural styles were *once* authentic even if they can no longer expect to be so.

After punk in Britain in 1976-7, these kinds of distinct subcultural groupings in 'white' youth culture have been few and far between. New Romantics (or Futurists/Blitz Kids) of the late 1970s and early 1980s seemed to some commentators like a synthesis of aspects of earlier subcultures, particularly 'glam', and attempts at 'alternative' lifestyles and bohemian attitudes to work reminiscent of the early hippies, whilst also harking back to the depressed economic climate of the 1930s – a sign seen as an appropriate echo in the depths of the new world recession which had been ushered in by the beginning of the new decade. When, later in the 1980s, goths emerged into the media spotlight with the chart success of bands such as The Mission, Fields of the Nephilim, All About Eve and the revamped, seminal, Sisters of Mercy, there was again a tendency to overemphasise the 'authentic' interpretation. Jon Savage, usually one of the more astute pop commentators of the decade, lapsed into this mode in part of a newspaper investigation into the 'new' goth phenomenon in 1987 when he claimed:

> Gothics tend to be local bright drop-outs from country towns and the provinces. They're often unemployed and dispossessed. Their style developed from a fusion of hippy and punk – more introverted than defiant. In general there is more gloom and doom in the north which may account for the popularity of this sub-cult up there. In London, it is ignored by all the style and pop media because it isn't a commercial fashion. It grew up from the grass roots.[4]

The roots of the production of such styles are not nearly so straightforward as these over-generalised comments would suggest. Heavy metal, Bowie and T-Rex – not to mention the Munsters television series – along with 'late' punk bands such as Souxsie and the Banshees, or early goth bands like Bauhaus, were more specific influences on the emergence of 1980s goth style. Further, the 'gloom and doom' image of the 'North' and the provinces in general is itself a cultural construct which reveals more about the metropolitan mass media than any geographical or sociological 'truths' about a locality. On the contrary, the Edinburgh-based Cut magazine began by selling to solely Scottish regions in the mid-1980s, but soon expanded to cover the territory north of Stoke-on-Trent on the assumption that there was an identity of consumer interest and pop tastes between youth in the North of England and in Scotland which was not shared by those in the (in its terms) 'backward' Midlands and the South. Increasingly in the 1980s bands and independent record companies and producers extolled the virtues of remaining in these 'marginal' areas of the kingdom rather than decamping to London despite the predominance of major record companies and media facilities in the capital. Further, a club like Manchester's Haçienda, part owned by members of New Order, contrived in its early years of existence at least, to play, ironically, with such a doom-laden iconography in its design style[5] and clientele. Initially in the late 1970s Joy Division, later to be renamed New Order, developed a following of 'serious looking young men with long grey overcoats' and, assisted by the much publicised death of singer Ian Curtis and the allegedly fascist connotations of band names and artwork, gave birth to a cult. Factory, their record label owned by television presenter (An)T(h)ony Wilson (associated with, So It Goes and The Other Side of Midnight, two of the prominent pop television series of the past twenty years), self-consciously recalled Andy Warhol and New York rather than the industrial Northern heartlands, but the imagery of grimy chimneys, work discipline and matchstick labourers was easily conjured, too. The Smiths, through Morrissey's obsessions with 1960s Northern 'realist' artefacts (like Viv Nicholson in Spend Spend Spend, and Coronation Street), made even more directly ironic commentary, in lyrical content and sleeve artwork, on the dour and doleful provincial lifestyle.

Post-punk white subcultures are, however, more difficult to fit into the lineage of post-war youth culture. Punk's playful, irreverent, attitude to the relationship between signifier and signified (Nazi insignia and fascism, or bondage gear and the sexual availability of women) prefigured a nation of youth at play – changing almost daily – with its desires and identities in the 1980s. For some more cautious New Deviancy, or Labelling, theorists, moreover, most youth are not, and never have been, 'in' subcultures – especially working class youth. Even if they are, writers like Stan Cohen argued, it is the worthlessness of job training, emptiness of education and lack of satisfactory work opportunities (which the liberal American subcultural theory of the 1950s and 1960s stressed most prominently) that seems most in evidence in contemporary youth subcultural choices. Resistance to dominant cultural values, or overt rebellion, was, in this more conventional explanation of youth, pop and deviance, confined to the middle class counter-culture of the late 1960s. Fatalism, not hope, then becomes, in this version of events, the most frequently encountered effect of mass (youth) unemployment which dominated the 1980s.

However, the experience of such economic and social catastrophe for the 'lost' or 'dispossessed' generation affected by the monetarist-inspired economic slump of 1980-2 is not so one-dimensional as New Deviancy theory suggests. For instance, such fatalistic practices as sitting glued to daytime television with its endless repeats of 1970s series is wryly parodied by bands such as Half Man, Half Biscuit, where the song 'I Hate Nerys Hughes (From The Heart)' took on the status of a political rallying cry. Having achieved independent chart success on the Probe Plus label, the band members went back to the dole determined to write a football fanzine for Third and Fourth Division League clubs, especially their beloved Tranmere Rovers. The band's most celebrated moment was indeed their refusal of a spot on Channel 4's pop show of the time, The Tube – produced in Newcastle – because its live transmission on a Friday night coincided with a Tranmere home fixture. William Hung and John Procter who make up the band I, Ludicrous developed this idiosyncratic style of ironic commentary on the mass media construction of popular culture even further, concentrating especially on soccer with songs such as 'Three English Football Grounds' and well signposted references to television sports commentators like David Coleman in 'Quite Extraordinary' and 'At The End of the Day'. Frank Sidebottom (along with Little Frank), the independent comedy eccentric from Timperley in Cheshire, has performed a similar role in celebrating non-League Altrincham, with 'The Robins Aren't Bobbins' and, more generally, 'All Time Great Footballing Chants'. These banal comments on the sheer banality of the media presentation of 'everyday life' emphasise the danger of doom-laden, knee-jerk sociological prophesies about the inevitable consequences of social, economic and technological change.

Cultural pessimism, however, is the most likely pitfall for youth culture analysis of the kind New Deviancy theorists have undertaken. Though thousands of youth styles walk the street today in a highly individualistic extravaganza, they are frequently read, or interpreted, as lacking in any radical political potential. Where once there was perceived to be a subversive, rebellious edge to such youth styles, since the early 1980s the dominant reading has been reversed. One prominent writer and broadcaster on deviance, Laurie Taylor, proclaimed in the *Times* in 1984 that the 'music has grown safe along with the culture', noting further the incorporation, as he saw it, of 'rebellious' youth styles into corporate advertising for customers. One instance was seen to be National Westminster Bank's widespread campaign in this period, promininently featuring spectacular youth styles as welcome potential customers. Under the sub-heading 'The Docile Generation', the byline sniped that 'Britain's youth, once thought unconventional and rebellious is no longer revolting. Neat hair, Mrs Thatcher and aerobics are in vogue. Even punk music has lost its drive; banks now aim their advertising at its followers.' Laurie Taylor's feature fitted into this mixture of nostalgia and pessimism, as he mused that:

> In place of all the simple rough disturbing amateurism of the original punk music, there is a new, controlled, self-preening professionalism. The soft punks and the new romantics and the alternatives and the posers (names for the new culture rise and fall with alacrity of chart entries) are massaged by music which depends for its impact as much upon producer as upon the artist. It is what one influential critic has described as the 'call of the mild' – the music made by Duran Duran, Boy George and Culture Club, and Spandau Ballet (now renamed by cynics, Spandau Wallet) . . . An equal concern with preening and individual self-image can be found among the followers.[6]

Also emphasised in this mode of youth culture analysis is the expression of a certain political attitude associated with youth and youth culture. Laurie Taylor specifically declared that he could find, in July 1984, 'no rebel rock here', quoting Boy George, at face value, as saying 'I am very conservative – And I love Coronation Street' though Taylor did acknowledge some significance in the 'gender-bending' of George, Marilyn and others. Similar arguments are constantly cited about the continued popularity (both on record and live tours) of 1970s 'progressive' rock music made by bands such as Pink Floyd, Genesis, and Yes: youth in the 1980s consuming such product were simply assumed to be doing so out of a sense of political and cultural conservatism.

Polling evidence on the youth vote in the 1980s suggested that Ronald Reagan's landslide re-election in 1984 was partly due to conservatism amongst American youth, and Margaret Thatcher's third term victory in June 1987 was seen to be ensured by young voters supporting her, defying stereotypes and psephological conventions, despite – or because of – Labour's self-consciously 'pop' youth campaign. The polls further questioned the significance of the emergence of Red Wedge[7] as one highly publicised strand of a Political Pop formation which had become identified in Britain since the previous General Election in 1983. Impressions of such a neo-conservatism in youth culture are, nevertheless, dangerously ambiguous: for example, soccer casuals partly subverted the uneven regional recession effects of so-called 'Thatcherism' by parading the *appearance* of wealth in the supposedly 'dull', 'grey', and 'gloomy' regions on match days.[8] These practices constituted a kind of respectability off the peg, but were – and indeed still are – frequently sustained by a criminal subculture and the black or 'casual' economy (exuding a menace, smartly and succintly captured by Latin Quarter in their lyrical snapshot 'No Ordinary Return' on their debut album). They were, too, inextricably connected to local economies and cultures. The persistent connection between Factory bands A Certain Ratio and, especially, archetypal scallies Happy Mondays and local football fans from the Greater Manchester region as well as the obsessive following of 'dinosaur' 1970s rock bands on Merseyside form part of another long running chapter in such a story which cannot be explained in terms of the 'resistance' of subcultural rituals.

Furthermore, a substantial focus of Britain's 'style wars' obsession has been on the upper-middle class who have benefitted most from the taxation policies of the new right in the United States of America and United Kingdom, and the de-regulation of financial and other sectors, especially in Britain. Advertising discourse pervaded this concern to spot, and create, new styles throughout the 1980s: yuppies, new georgians, young fogies, sloanes and so on have been in one sense grist to business consultancies run by style-pundits such as Peter York. York's one-time radicalism rapidly became simplistic self-parody. A poem written by scally-wag 'Joe Average' in the Merseyside fanzine *The End* in 1987, greeted a lecture by York on ITV's South Bank Show – to a narrowly selected studio audience – in typically derisory fashion:

Peter York you make me sick
You smug, self righteous, Sloane Ranger prick
You talk about trends, fashion and style,
But all it really is, is verbal bile.
You adore the rich and aristocrats, too.

Hanging by your bollocks is too good for you.
You play with words and generalise
People like you, I really despise.
You lecture to hand-picked prats
on the South Bank Show
Why didn't they give you stick, I just don't know.
Post modernism, post industrial and Post War
If the truth be known you're just a bore.
You've made talking bullshit into a fine art
You pretentious, patronising, spoon-fed, fart.

This End-piece may represent an extreme version of the popular response but there is no doubt that Style Culture, rather than signifying a new youth subculture, rapidly became a figure in an advertising discourse which has been read, and responded to, in various contradictory ways. The main 'style' magazines, including *Arena*, male audience offshoot of *The Face*, have been consistently cited as instances of the growing hold of Style Culture over certain aspects of pop music and youth culture. This hegemony, however, is too frequently assumed rather than demonstrated. The metropolitan bias of such instances of Style Culture is highly significant. To some extent, pop music culture's genesis has always been a product of the periphery/centre dichotomy, rather than the subculture/culture explanation.[9]

For instance, the North of England's most critical cultural magazine, since its inception in November 1983, was *Debris*. This politically acerbic fan/magazine, was mainly run by Dave Haslam, disc jockey at clubs like the Haçienda and Isadora's, and joint owner of the independent Play Hard record company. Play Hard has had on its list, amongst others, The Bodines, King of the Slums, Kit, The Train Set, Benny Profane and MC Buzz B, and was responsible for the one of the best vinyl representations of what we have termed here Post-Political Pop; the 1987 *Head Over Ears* compilation album issued with a special number of the magazine. Despite a sales figure of only three thousand, *Debris*, like other examples of this genre, had a pervasive effect on musical tastes, organisation and styles way beyond its initial readership. Its editorial view, expressed in issue 11, of *The Face* as a 'bag of expensive sick only read these days by Californian college kids, Tories and Japanese schoolchildren' captured something of the cynicism and ambivalence expressed towards Style Culture by many of the consumers who have been generally presumed to be its disciples. Readers of *The Face*, and the then newly redesigned Labour Party monthly theoretical journal *New Socialist* were simply assumed to be languishing under the spell of Neville Brody's graphic design revolution, and Robert Elms' brattish prose (Elms' article 'Ditching the Drabbies' had already provoked a stormy debate with David Edgar and others, who defended a visibly withering 1960s political and countercultural legacy). This analysis, was underlined by an incisive interview, in issue 17 in 1988, with the widely respected music reviewer David Toop, which claimed that 'most months his column is the only thing worth reading in *The Face*' (apart from the occasional James Truman and Penman on film)'. Haslam also pointed, in issue 15 in

1987, on the occasion of the British General Election of that year, to what he saw as the insidious connection between Style Culture and youth culture. He argued that:

> Our society has turned right, and the edge of the cliff is just a step away.... there's the horrific sight of the youth culture politicos of our generation; Red Wedge, Robert Elms, Attila the Stockbroker, Sarah Jane Morris, and Paul Weller. Red Wedge whinge, the Stockbroker swears, and Weller wears some neat new trousers and . . . inspiration ? (with the probable exception of Jerry Dammers) there is none. . . Youth culture seems to be travelling the same way, to the same cliff edge, as the rest of our society ... And we get left in front of the TV all day watching the world entertain us.

This passage – perhaps understandably given the political context of the period – displays a more 'ranting' style of writing than *Debris* generally employed to critically map the formations of 1980s youth and pop music culture. Whether in his regular contributions to the *New Musical Express* in 1986 and 1987, or in magazines such as *City Life* and M62 as well as *Debris*, and in television interviews, Haslam's arguments consistently displayed a thoughtful critique of the discourses which constitute contemporary pop culture. Indeed, one of his 'beefs about commentators' on pop culture 'is that what they say isn't reflective enough'. He can, he says, 'excuse Julie Burchill for the way she writes because in a way the way she writes actually is closer to a truth about pop culture...because her's is straight off the top of her head, very brash, very now, very today.' Haslam would distinguish some brands of cultural criticism as separate from this 'pop culture process' which demands that 'if you want to have influence then you write like her'. Julie Burchill's own political trajectory from teenage punk journalist on the *New Musical Express* in the 1970s to columnist for the right-wing press in the 1980s tells its own story, but Haslam's argument that the 'power of the written word', despite the prospect of a small readership for fan/magazines, is still capable of expressing 'deeper' historical realities, rather than merely reflecting the 'fact that everything is just dispensable' still holds good. For Haslam, many pop culture commentators 'never actually get to the nitty gritty of why a band is good and when you're dealing with music that is the first question: why is Roxanne Shante more important than Cliff Richard? In sociological terms Cliff Richard is more important, more people go to his gigs and yet as a DJ, as a music fan, as a writer it's my responsibility to say exactly why Roxanne Shante is better than Cliff Richard.'

Further, this debate about the (un)truths and philoso contagion of Style Culture is not just a matter of contemporary record. For Dave Haslam:

if you write today's story accurately and well, you're writing tomorrow's history, and that's why I still harbour real anger about just plain inaccuracy in music journalism. And you only realise that when you're actually part of the music business and you realise that what the NME says is not infallible, not just as far as judgemental terms goes but as far as fact goes, and that they can say this and this and this is happening ground, when you're working in that city, you might know that this and this and this has happened, or might one day happen, but isn't actually what is good, and what is the essence of that city.'

The inaccuracy, for Haslam:

comes out of pop commentators wanting everything in black and white, and if you want to simplify things, if you want to say this is the Manchester scene, and you want to say it in anything less than three volumes, then you're going to misrepresent what is happening, and if you're going to say it in 500 words in the NME then you're doing a total disservice to the city, and to history.'[10]

This misconception, Haslam identifies generally, as a 'by-product of a method that people use in order to address pop culture; by making it black and white and by ignoring the complexity of it then you're misrepresenting it.' It is indeed the problem of the method of addressing the object of pop culture which is at the heart of the debate over youth culture and Style Culture. Football/music fanzines rather than music/political fanzines are the prime example of this. They emerged (with the exception of early one-club role models such as York's *Terrace Talk* and Bradford City's *City Gent*) and then mushroomed in the mid-1980s, especially from late 1985, as soccer's decaying relationship to its consumers was compounded by media ineptitude in coverage of the Bradford, Heysel and Hillsborough stadium disasters and subsequent government 'moral panics' and 'law and order' campaigns culminating in the Football Spectators Act, 1989, Part 1 of which contained the infamous identity card proposal.

As Simon Frith has put it in a comment on pop music culture, 'pop fanzines capture the *enthusiasm* of consumption'.[11] It is exactly the same in this soccer subculture. The astonishing, and entirely unpredicted, rise in number of football fanzines in Britain since 1984 reflects a similar practice amongst young soccer fans – mainly males in their twenties and thirties. A spirit of mutual co-operation and collectivism, despite inevitable over-dependence on particular individuals, has been a difficult guiding principle to maintain: as far as it is possible to judge so far, criteria such as agreement not to criticise each other's magazines in print, writing for complementary fanzines, and helping to set up new fanzines have remained uppermost in many, though not all, contributions to the debates. The 'do-it-yourself' ethos of football fanzines is reminiscent of punk in its early days, and much of the inspiration is undoubtedly from that era. *The End* is one early archetypal 1980s example, eventually mixing music and clothes as well as soccer in its subject matter, but for the vast majority football became virtually the sole source of concern. The problem for the network of fanzines around the cultural industries of soccer and popular music is the same one that faced the likes of *Sniffin' Glue* (the 'original' punk fanzine in many ways) in the aftermath of punk.

To enthuse about the 'product' to be consumed – whether it is football, music, clothes or whatever – however critically, implies some kind of support for the industry that produces the commodities for our multiple pleasures. Fanzines attached to particular clubs, at least loosely, have to cope with the extra burdens of not overstepping the mark of criticism. To be worthwhile they have to be able to ask questions of the organisation's day-to-day management without being perceived as too offensive, in case the football club imposes a ban on sales on the terraces or around the ground on match days, as has sometimes occurred. They are also overwhelmingly male-dominated (despite the existence of *Balls*, the football fanzine world's answer to sexist chants like 'Get Your Tits Out for the Lads') and the difficulty of sustaining initial bursts of enthusiasm and flair without blunting the sharpness of their vitriolic pens is ever-present.

It is wit and inventiveness, though, which mark the best of them; *When Saturday Comes*, the most widely read and praised of all, paid homage to an Undertones song in its title, whilst *When Sunday Comes* registered – obliquely – the fact that Liverpool FC appear so regularly on live televised matches. The quality of the football fanzines (by late 1989 numbering over two hundred in Britain and Ireland) is inevitably variable but their courageous sense of hedonistic fun in the face of widespread official proclamations of the deviance of *all* football supporters, not to mention legislative intervention to enforce the carrying of compulsory membership cards, gives sustenance to campaigns to democratise the industry. As Simon Reynolds – writing in *Monitor* about fanzines in general – argued, what 'is significant about fanzines is not what they say so much as what they are, or even *that* they are . . . Fanzine rhetoric is not the promise but the substance of change.'[12] By just 'being there' such fanzines have marked out a local terrain around soccer and pop music culture which constitutes a different object, and a different mode of address, from that of the global media. They have, further, distinguished themselves in the main from the racist and fascist English football hooligan subculture which has hardened and broadened its influence on the international stage throughout the Thatcher years. These ugly reminders of the brutalising effects of a post-Empire in decline ('Thatcher's boys', as we have christened them elsewhere) intertwine with neo-fascist music bands and record outlets, increasingly organised on a European-wide basis.

However, there are limited possibilities for any kind of subcultural politics to be built around pop music culture. The term Style Culture symbolised a decade which witnessed extremely volatile affinities and identities and contradictory shifts in production and consumption of commodities in the leisure and culture industries, such as soccer and popular music. Anti-racist alliances of the late 1970s, such as the Anti-Nazi League and Rock Against Racism, comprise one model based on adoption of a strategy which pitched teds, punks, skins, mods, rastas and others into a (then) newly formative politics of youth. Despite achievement of many of its objectives in a limited arena (for instance, countering the influence of the National Front, British Movement and other right-wing groups in cultural activities like soccer and pop music) there was always the suspicion that underneath a badge of unity there was support for Two Tone bands like The Selector, Jerry Dammers' Specials and The Beat *alongside* a commitment to, or even membership of, the targeted enemy – fascist organisations themselves.[13] Conditions of possibility of such alliances receded even further in the decade after Rock Against Racism, as a result of government policies – in the United Kingdom at least – which managed to translate what were then more marginal ideologies around race and immigration into contemporary state practice.

In some ways the more pessimistic readings of the stylistic moods and nuances of active post-punk subcultures stems from an over-optimistic and one-dimensional theorisation of youth culture in the past three or four decades. Such orthodoxies, despite the innovatory and far reaching effects of the most incisive of this theoretical work, have paved the way for the rhetoric which now dominates discussion of youth culture. That is, that the historical line of development of youth subcultures, whether the starting point is taken to be 1945, or the last century, has come to a (permanent) halt, leaving only the alternatives of either wallowing in a retro-pop nostalgia for a golden past, or else deepening the left and right cynicism which permeates current cultural politics.

The times of the signs

There are other clear limitations to subcultural analysis, exposed both by the profound change in the context of the generation and proliferation of youth styles today and also by the lack of cohesion between the theoretical terms and ethnographic or impressionistic snapshots. One route out of the morass of youth culture and subculture theory has been to heed the injunction to concentrate on what young people 'actually do', such as hanging round street corners, listening to records, drinking, having sex, watching videos, and ba-bysitting[14] rather than reading in some formalised codes to these practices derived from past youth culture and youth subculture mythology. Another strategy has been to depart from the the orthodox belief that ethnographies would help to reveal the mode in which subcultural groups experience shifts in social relations and ideologies over any particular historical period. Instead, the focus for theoretical analysis has started to become *musical* rather than subcultural styles. Hip-hop, house, folk/punk, jazz, ska or heavy metal is then the realm of inquiry in the first instance, not the sorts of subcultures assumed to be associated with the appropriate musical forms. There has further been a tendency to read these musical styles strictly (like fashion) as a text – as if they were structured like a language. Subcultures are, then, in this theoretical account, decipherable through the message of the medium. This tendency has progressed from its mid-1970s positions which relied on the use by Paul Willis[15] of the concept of 'homology' to account for the perceived fit between subcultural 'givens' such as drugs, musical and sexual preference, choice of dress styles, transport and language. However, as far as subcultural analysis is concerned, this approach may highlight even more problems with the initial sub-culturalist predilections so as to lead to the abandonment of their central concepts altogether. In fact, the most telling criticism of these basic assumptions about youth subcultures is their association with a view, embedded in rock theory, that rock music is in itself 'radical and oppositional'.[16]

It is not, then, so much that youth culture died in the 1980s; more that its position as a subject of conflicting historical discourses in specific cultural formations is radically shifting, as was noted in Chapter 1. The Centre for Contemporary Cultural Studies tradition theorised subcultures as forms of 'resistance through rituals' to changes in the dominant culture, in a succession of phases since the early 1950s. The view enshrined in these Cultural Studies texts that subcultural styles developed first as street styles then as 'high-street' styles, however, gives too much credence to the notion of subculture as a self-generating process. It helped to pave the way for some major misreadings of styles, identities and sexualities associated with punk and post-punk youth culture, and the possibilities of transformation of them in the present. Most of all it cemented the idea of rock music culture as counter-culture, failing to interrogate the complex of discourses and practices which made that particular nexus of music, politics and lifestyle in the late 1960s. Consequently, new bohemian formations both in the 1980s and 1990s are in danger of being hailed for what they are not, but also of being underestimated; of being taken for granted as merely yet another revival of 'originals' which, by comparison, are 'still the greatest'.

A useful contemporary instance of this is hip-hop, perhaps the only youth subculture since punk to attain a worldwide status. Its genesis has been, in one writing – and reading – of its history, a model of subcultural formation: from the (initially American) street to television advertising parlance in ten easy lessons, with the usual media hype on theft, drug-taking, violence and other juvenile delinquency at concerts thrown in. Identikit pen pictures soon displayed rap crews dressed in collective homeboy style right down to laceless Adidas trainers – satirised neatly on cover of the London label's Various Artists *Christmas Rap* in 1987, featuring a packaged and parcelled (wrapped) rapper with only these essential items showing. It is a mistake, however, to substitute hip-hop – or Acid House for that matter – as the new punk, and carry on with the analysis of youth culture as before. Theoretical accounts in academic disciplines such as criminology and sociology, which have positioned, conceptually, youth culture and youth subculture in a relation of resistance to, or rebellion towards, a 'dominant culture' have sustained and developed a notion of rock culture as resistant or rebellious, too. Such notions are not capable of capturing the changes in youth culture and rock culture from at least the late 1970s onwards. They are, moreover, unsatisfactory, as accounts of pop history and youth culture in general. It is, instead, the musical form rather than the youth style which matters most in the politics of hip-hop, as with any other contender for punk's successor. The focus has already been shifted to the production, distribution and exchange of musical rather than merely 'life' styles by the policing, regulation and reorganisation of the cultural industries themselves. But there needs to be, too, a history of the shift in relations of what we might call Pop Time and Pop Space which are now occurring.

Pop since the 1950s has constantly been used as a 'sign' of the times. The sense of post-war cultural history in Britain in particular is deeply dependent on the supposed evocation of particular periods of time by specific snatches of popular sonic history. Rock'n'roll is thus taken – of necessity contentiously – to 'represent' the mid-late 1950s; the Beatles' early singles to signify the mid-1960s; punk to recall the mid-1970s; Bruce Springsteen's *Born In The USA* album to stand for the mid-1980s, and so on. However, artistic production in any cultural medium in the 1980s and 1990s could be seen as no longer in 'tune' with the period in which it was made. It has even been contended that it is precisely this dislocation of an art form from the social, economic and cultural context that produced it which mark out our contemporary condition.[17]

For some writers, Jean Baudrillard's postmodernist theory of the crisis of what he refers to as the 'social' – especially of the 'implosion' of meaning – is applicable to such an account of pop history. As an example, John McDonald, in commenting on Baudrillard's work, argues that we 'can see strong evidence for Baudrillard's theories of social implosion in the increasing formularisation of pop music in recent years. This is is not to contend that things were so much better or more original 15-20 years ago. Originality is unquantifiable, and in practice something of a romantic blind alley.' More pointedly, McDonald also draws on Roland Barthes' notion of the 'grain of the voice' which denotes the body in the voice as it sings, the hand as it writes, the limb as it performs. McDonald suggests that:

> What we can detect is a change in the *grain* of popular music in the sense that Barthes talks of 'the grain of the voice'. Pop music may not have been any less formularised in the sixties but it wasn't so resolutely enclosed and controlled by a network of media hype and marketing strategies. There was more room for experimentation, a slower escalation and exhaustion of successful sub-genres, and a much more limited turnover of prepackaged

nostalgias. These differences must inevitably be reflected in the music itself.

While it can be recognised that pop music culture is increasingly 'becoming an inward-spiralling game of references' (hence the call upon the Baudrillardian theme of 'implosion'), the extent to which a 'punk bohemia' provided a watershed in this version of pop history is questionable. McDonald claims that:

> The only interruption to the smooth mechanisation of the pop industry came with the entry of punk rock in the mid to late seventies. Punk brought in a burst of energy which temporarily upset the complacency of record companies, musicians and consumers, though this small triumph only served eventually to make the industry more seamless and complete. It took only a short space of time until the so-called 'new wave' had been popularised and disseminated everywhere in various watered-down guises, until no semblance of revolt was possible in such a musical expression; all punk iconography had been effectively neutralised and incorporated into the body of the social. Ironically punk's greatest impact took place precisely after its moment of genuine vitality had passed. The hard core original punk was of necessity a marginal phenomenon, only the sign of this marginality remains in today's new-wave styles that have come to dominate every aspect of pop culture. Punk had to die to be born – and acquire its social exchange value.

In some ways this is a provocative but perplexing argument on Baudrillardian lines. There would certainly have to be allowance made for the uneven effect of punk's shock waves in different regions of the globe and account taken of the fact that McDonald's critical essay emanated from Australia in 1984. Nevertheless, despite its usefulness this ultimately remains a dubious reading of punk's significance. It accords too much credence to the idea that punk was the *only* high point in a linear view of pop history, and assumes that everything coming after this peak was merely trough. However, McDonald does move nearer to the nub of punk's legacy when he writes that:

> What we are left with now is a pop music in which the ideas of sensation and revolution have been structurally excluded. Just as art has never been able to better the outrages of the Dadaists, so too is pop unable to be genuinely shocking in any way and not be simply written off as 'punk' – a well-defined sub-genre that always fits certain behavioural expectations.[18]

There are a number of other problems with this kind of theorisation of pop music culture which attempts to utilise the work of Baudrillard. These will be considered later in the book. At this juncture it needs to be emphasised that what would distinctively mark out a different writing of pop history from the multitude already produced is an approach in which there is a re-consideration of Pop Time. The distinguishing characteristics of pop in the contemporary world are not the rise and fall of stars like Bananarama, Terence Trent D'Arby and Madness or producers like Stock-Aitken-Waterman and Steve Lillywhite. They all have their earlier equivalents. Nor is (post)modernity in the popular music industry necessarily signified by the new phenomenon of 'pop around the clock' music video formats. It is rather the rapidly changing velocity of Pop Time – the speed at which things come around again in the circular time scales of fashionability – and the context or 'space' in which the musical commodities are produced and consumed which carve out a particularly important, and possibly prophetic, place for pop as a site of contemporary cultural politics. As the markets for popular music and associated commodities, and the legal rights to their exploitation, progressively expand, pop history itself becomes more fragile. At the same time, there is *less* chance than ever before of bands or artists making a 'name' for themselves, of 'making pop history'; or if they do achieve fame, there is less time in which to do so, less time 'at the top'. The nature of pop and rock discourse today, and especially the challenge to prevailing rock theory of such developments, is such that replacements and challengers for current stars exists, literally, all over the world. Pop and rock subjects and objects are everwhere.

Rap and hip-hop are again the prime example rather than, as some postmodernist theorists of postmodernism have argued, punk (or even avant-garde) bands. Much rap and hip-hop now *denies* 'history', even its own empirical history[19] from African jive to New York to Manchester. Hip-hop, has increasingly, consisted of a specific development of the commodity form, quite separate from the play of punk or glam. Cutting across gender lines, more and more hip-hop product has consisted of the ethos: ' I'm here, I'm the best, Buy *Me*'. The urgency of a post-Aids, postmodern scene is writ large in hip-hop. Just as rock and pop culture is shifting its significance in the various discourses and practices which underwrite it, hip-hop adopts – even becomes – the slogan 'I sell therefore I am'. Further, as pop history seems ever shorter (it is, conceivably, the 'end of' pop history, to plunder Baudrillard) a place in pop's hall of fame is now available, if at all, for a split second. Meanwhile, the global markets for pop and rock commodities grow ever wider. In that sense, there will be no 'Beatles of hip-hop'. Moreover, as Dave Haslam argues, one reason for this is that:

the people who grew up enjoying the Beatles and the Rolling Stones are now forty or fifty and they're actually the people who are still in control of the music industry. To them there will never be another Beatles, there will never be another Rolling Stones – the main reason is because they will never be a teenager again. And therefore they have no need for another Beatles. Why discover another Beatles if you can sell the Beatles boxed set in a *wooden* box at Christmas time? Its a paradox as far as the industry is concerned. They still need product, new product, but they don't want it to turn the whole world upside down. They're quite happy to be able to sell house music because they also own shares in Smiley T-shirt manufacturers but they don't actually want Acid House to destroy everything that's gone before and start year zero with the 'Summer of '88'.

It is, however, not the case that the 'speed' of Pop Time is itself a new problem in the politics of pop, or that the velocity is necessarily to be seen in terms of linear time – in other words, not all elements of crossover (from 'margin' to mainstream, from underground club scene to chart success, from one fad to the next) can be explained simply by being more ephemeral than their predecessors of five, ten or fifteen years ago. As Dave Haslam further points out:

there is a *constant* need of pop culture to say this is new, and these circumstances have never before prevailed. But this is an illusion, and in fact nothing is new – it isn't new at all. But the industry needs to think its new because the writers need to say "this is happening *now*". Major labels need new things to discover and thus to sell, and tired old rock musicians need new producers so that they can go into the studio and remix their track, so it appears new. And that's always been true.

To the extent that the speed of this process has accelerated, it is, for Haslam, 'because desperation has increased and therefore increased the need to speed up. Who are the people with their foot on the accelerator speeding up pop culture? To me it is the wrong people.'

This is shown in specific musical hypes: in Acid House and the 'Summer of Love', in particular. Haslam contends that this is particularly true as regards:

the 'Acid' revolution say. Whereas the hip-hop revolution of the year before was, I think, more influential in studio techniques, in types of sound, in breaking down barriers between different ghettos of people and opening up whole new types of music to people. Without hip-hop, Acid wouldn't have had anywhere to go. And yet hip-hop wasn't quite what the producers wanted because there was something about it they didn't quite like, the music wasn't quite radio playable, the sound was a bit too rough and the things that people were saying wasn't quite right. There was no kind of – apart from Adidas wear

– there wasn't really a whole lifestyle to sell. So therefore when Acid came along everyone thought 'oh, we'd better not make the mistake we did of ignoring hip-hop, let's go for broke.' And all of a sudden you had a whole lifestyle, and people said that's what we want.

Rock around the block

This vexed question of the velocity of the process of change in pop history necessarily involves the notion of the 'absolute power of the instant', where, another influential theorist of postmodernity, Paul Virilio, has argued, we are witnessing the 'dwindling of the last commodity: duration'.[20] For Virilio, unlike Baudrillard, politics needs to be re-established not to be allowed to 'disappear'. The requirement in adequately accounting for the policing and regulating of pop music culture is indeed for a politics which takes 'speed' into account, since the most significant characteristic of our age is, as Virilio claims, the 'depletion of time'. In a comment which encapsulates the shifts in Pop Time perfectly, Virilio says, in his interviews with Sylvere Lotringer, of time in general that history 'as the extensiveness of time – of time that lasts, is portioned out, organised, developed – is disappearing in favour of the instant, as if the end of history were the end of duration in favour of instantaneousness, and of course, of ubiquity.'[21]

The twin factors of time's reduction to an instant, but being *everywhere*, are precisely the facets of pop and rock music culture which should attract our critical attention in the age of instantaneous electronic communication, whether it be for Stock Markets, sporting events or pop concerts. The 'socially conscious', or 'protest' aspects of Political Pop amount to a part of a social formation given global dimension at television gatherings like Nelson Mandela's 70th Birthday Party or Live Aid. They are also prime instances of Virilio's notion that geographical space (a city, Wembley stadium) has been displaced by a 'concentration in broadcasting time. Broadcasting replaces urbanisation. It's a city of the instant in which a billion people are gathered.'[22]

Subcultural theorists' readings of Sport Aid, Live Aid or Mandela's Birthday Party have tended to reclaim them as 'People Aid', as representative of a new, more optimistic politics sweeping the land, particularly amongst 'youth'. However, as we have seen, subcultural theory emanated and developed from a politics which designated an 'authenticity' to 'street' – and by implication popular music – styles which, literally, had a point or place of historical origin. For Baudrillard, Virilio, and other theorists of postmodern 'travel' and 'tourism' such placement is always a problem. As the Australian cultural critic Meaghan Morris argues, 'there is no such "place" to start with'.[23] The 'street' in Britain, or the 'boxcar' or the 'road' in the United States of America, are mythical constructs of popular cultural practices. For youth culture, too, such myths have frequently been highly gendered: in other words, the 'street' has often been seen as a male domain, the 'bedroom' a female one – though Morrissey's claims to have lived a hermit's existence could also be taken to reflect the desires and tentative masculinities of thousands of his contemporaries.

Nevertheless, space is of particular importance in understanding the shifts in the cultural politics of pop in the postmodern world. Canadian writer Jody Berland has shown that although 'music is thought of as a purely time-based art (inaccurately, as some contemporary musical performance demonstrates)', it is 'not time that resonates, or class, or even "content", but space: experienced as both metaphorical (that which is thought, overcome, lost in, settled into) and physical (that which is discovered, traversed, expanded, conquered)'.[24] Furthermore, for such theorists, it is possible to claim that we 'are all interpellated as members of discursive communities whose locations are multiple and even contradictory; simultaneously domesticated and internationalised, isolated and ubiquitously surrounded, here and somewhere not placed, voting with ballots in one country and record sales in another, fans of 'The World' we are and are not in.'[25]

It is in such complex relations across the local/global fault lines of time and space that the changing meaning and contours of rock, pop and youth culture is to be found in the 'postmodern condition'. Whatever could have been said of pop's past, this is manifestly now post-subcultural pop.

3

Soundtracks from the global hypermarket: post-pop politics

In the first two Chapters we have examined the case for subcultural theorists' explanations of post-punk pop music culture. Subcultural theory has been found wanting in such accounts; it is more than likely that it was similarly inadequate in its analysis of pre-punk subcultures, too. Moreover, the notion of Style Culture, which dominated subcultural politics of pop in the early part of the decade, was seriously misleading. Where it retained lasting value – for instance in its links with the early 1980s warehouse scene which eventually hosted the 'horrors' of Acid House parties – subcultural theory was an inappropriate discourse to draw upon. In addition to subcultural theory, in the next two Chapters we also need to consider the contribution of an alternative set of inquiries, largely stemming from literary theory.

A shift occurred in rock theory and pop sensibility in the 1980s which posed a number of problems for the contemporary cultural politics of pop. One manifestation of this shift, which has been confusingly read as an example of a new 'authenticity', has, as we have seen, been the re-development of socially conscious, or protest pop. Another has been the emergence of 'New Age' culture and music, a label which encompasses the experimental 'ambient' work of former Roxy Music star Brian Eno and former Velvet Underground stalwart John Cale through to guitarist Michael Chapman and keyboard player Rick Wakeman who have past associations with counter-cultural and 'progressive' rock movements in the 1960s and early 1970s, along with a wave of newer singers and players. Even those 1960s artists who have no formal connection to New Age, like Van Morrison, frequently come close to it in their musical sound and social philosophies. Nick Austin, founder of a premier New Age label, Coda, has described his sudden 'discovery' in America:

> that there was a new form of music somewhere between classical and pop that was breaking through an otherwise pop orientated industry without the usual media hype. I subsequently resolved to go to the States to find out more

about this kind of music with a view to introducing it to the British and European public ... Contrary to expectations I found that New Age music is now one of the largest growth areas in American record business second only to compact discs and started several years ago through what Americans call alternative distribution. By this they mean alternative non-traditional record outlets - bookstores, university campus shops, mail order, and word of mouth ... Because New Age music is usually instrumental in nature by American definition instrumental albums must be Jazz. To British ears New Age could hardly be called Jazz. It has an appeal that is broadly speaking from Eno to Elgar but with one important difference. All New Age artists are still very much alive. New Age music has strong acoustic connections breaking away from the pop values that determine today's usual charts. New Age music relies heavily on melody, the values of being able to play an instrument to evoke an atmosphere or emotion.

We have, so far, described the instances of New Age and protest pop, amongst other pop moods, in terms of a more general formation, Political Pop, which, whilst allowing for competing claims of other modes of constructing pop's social, economic and political importance, has tended to predominate since the period of New Pop. The link between what are seemingly disparate facets of the markets generated by the international popular music industry is their rejection of the 'pop' (and subcultural) politics which characterised the period and style of New Pop. To the extent that they try to reinject politics into pop they do so based on other criteria, derived mainly from a combination of rock and folk ideologies. For 'protest', 'radical' or 'revolutionary' pop this means a commitment to the correctness of the song's line, or else the authenticity of the musical form (Paul Weller and the Style Council's preference for soul, Sting's bias towards jazz). For New Age or associated styles it means an ability to represent 'true' emotions with specific combination of carefully arranged instruments and voices.

The focus of this book is also the Post-Political Pop which has developed in relationship to Political Pop in the era of the 'countercultures'. That is not to suggest that it is necessarily historically *after* Political Pop; in some senses it has predated Political Pop – in the same way that some theorists (Jean-François Lyotard in particular) have argued that postmodernism is more properly seen as the founding moment of modernism. Therefore, to understand Post-Political Pop as a social formation, it is important to gauge how the genre of Political Pop has evolved: what kinds of practices and discourses have been mobilised and what conditions allowed such a turn in the pop labelling process to come about? Here, the idea, popular in the rock ideology of the 1960s, that rock can be seen as a kind of folk music which *expresses* the interests and values of a community is a key notion to interrogate.

One of the problems which emerges from an analysis of this specific pop mode is that of application and specification of terms within literary theory, especially 'realism'. Some aspects of the folk ideology which have been drawn upon stress folk protest as a direct, unmediated, and therefore 'authentic' expression of real needs, desires and feelings. It is then set against 'inauthentic' protest: rap and hip-hop, for example, are sometimes excluded, sometimes included, on these grounds. An instance of this folk purity argument, especially in connection with black music, was displayed starkly in the editorial of the first issue of *British Blues Review* (the official journal of the British Blues Network) in April 1988, which informed its readers that:

> Blues music, an anachronism based on cover versions of a musical era now defunct, is incomprehensible to the masses, while the knowledgeable teeter on the brink of self-indulgence. Why bother? Hip Hop, Rap, and associated crutt – that's why! Show you care – buy a bluesman a drink, this week, and help preserve the species.

In other words, 'black' (blues) music was authentic when it was pure, unmediated by commercial reward, and sung from the heart of poor America, but when young blacks make money out of it (for instance in hip-hop) it is somehow inauthentic. Robert Cray's sophisticated resurrection of the 1960s fusion of Stax soul and Chicago blues forms set in a slick, stylish context met similar criticism as he almost single-handedly headed the blues' commercial revival in the 1980s. However, what needs examination is the inadequacies of this kind of explanation, and an exploration of alternatives. The construction of identities, the shaping of desire, are much more pertinent issues in establishing the workings of the old and new forms of authenticity. In Roland Barthes' terms, as has been seen already, it is the 'grain of the voice' – the body in the voice as it sings, or the *materiality* of the body – which requires attention not the simple lyrical realism of the words on a page. How contemporary soul singers like Anita Baker, Luther Vandross or Melis'a Morgan say what they mean is as important as knowing that they mean what they say.

Contrary to much pop culture criticism based on literary theory, notions of rebellion and resistance, or truthfulness and honesty of emotion, cannot be directly read from the lyrical correctness of songs. Calls amongst rock theorists for new music which 'would capture and extend the emerging political consciousness' taken to be reflected in, for instance, what American writer Michael Omi calls the 'Charity Rock Phenomenon', oversimplify the interconnectedness between musical forms and the ideological communities they seek to represent. The 'Rare Groove' or 'Modern Soul' movements, for example, carry on the spirit of 1970s Northern Soul of Wigan Casino and Blackpool Mecca Ballroom without, in any simplistic way, reviving the music and politics of those former youth subcultures.

It is, instead, the historical development of pop as one of the major sites of cultural politics today which needs to be considered, not the contorted pursuance of flawed thinking in rock theory. The insistence by Omi that 'rock is an extremely powerful medium among the youth of this country, perhaps *the* most powerful',[1] and that a politics of rock can be formulated on such a notion, is an inadequate response to the historical changes in rock and pop discourse of the post-war world.

The hyperreal thing

The Bruce Springsteen phenomenon, especially his renowned 'live' performances[2] displays many of the contradictions concerning the return of rock ideology. His international tour of 1985 summed up the major difficulties. 'Born in the USA' was a strong contender for the year's anthem, a song about the prolonged horrors of Vietnam, a parable which Bobbie Ann Mason's novel, *In Country*, takes up in a brilliant fictional espousal of the chord which such Springsteen epics might be supposed to strike. Yet it took on the persona of a musical Rambo; its sales were massive, and nothing could stop the Boss as country after country succumbed to the marathon stage performances. Everywhere 'Born in the USA' appeared like a hymn to the mother country, a restatement that the 'US is best'. While the spate of Vietnam movies helped to erase the memory of the war in film culture, Springsteen assisted in restoring American dominance on the stages of Europe, signalling the end of the hegemony of the 'hip little Englanders'[3] of New Pop.

This marked the conclusion of the second British invasion of American pop, recalling the pattern of the first such sortie by the likes of The Beatles, Rolling Stones, Herman's Hermits and Dave Clark Five in the 1960s. Once again the aggressive 'don't fuck with me' American eagle flew proudly over the globe alongside McDonalds and Dallas. Whilst Springsteen as an individual, in his lifestyle and lyrics, championed the blue-collar male ideology giving thousands of pounds to labour movement groups like the British miners, it was traditional American Pie – strong, assertive, loud and proud – that ensured his eventual elevation to megastar status after so many years of being 'on the road' since the early 1970s.

In what could be seen as a forerunner of many of the constituent elements of Political Pop, CBS released Springsteen's 'minimalist' *Nebraska* album in 1982. A bare, stripped, downbeat folk record, taped on his own machine, it was seen in at least one reading[4] as Reaganite in its description of a world where misfortune and hardship simply occurred randomly; where no attribution of blame to state or political party could be made. 'Born in the USA' turned out to be the upbeat, band, version of this narrative of mythical America. Springsteen's importance in the transformations which led to Political Pop was not his folk representation of a disposessed community (Vietnam vets, poor farmers, sacked or striking workers) but his symbolisation of the 'real'. His part in the resuscitation of rock ideology was pointed to by Adrian Martin and Gerard Hayes in their account of the 'Eighties':

> Old instruments return – in themselves arbitrary, but the announcement of their triumphant revival burdens them with a sorry socio-cultural significance. The heavy metal guitar, the blues harmonica and – god help us – *real* drums. Molly Meldrum went quite ecstatic on *Countdown* when he proclaimed the return of Bruce Springsteen, the living spirit of rock'n'roll, with these words: 'Good on ya, Bruce – real drums!'[5]

Real instruments were seen to go along with real feelings in Springsteen's rise: a certain sort of musical and artistic purity going hand in hand with a sincere message. Martin and Hayes decried this combination of 'rockin energy and political authenticity', but they alighted on exactly the bases of Springsteen's rock power which go way beyond the frequent bombast of the music itself.

The sharp contrast with Springsteen's commercial rock triumphs in the years after 1984 is provided by the simultaneous decline of Frankie Goes To Hollywood.[6] A postscript was also provided by Holly Johnson's solo battle hymn to the republic in 'Americanos' where he sang the praises of 'blue jeans and chinos'. In the summer before 'Born in the USA' eventually took the international pop world by storm (although the album of the same name had initially been released to much less acclaim in 1984), Frankie said – through T-shirt overkill – that we should 'arm the unemployed'. Through 'Relax' and 'Two Tribes', two massively successful chart singles, sexual politics and anti-war protest were enshrined in legacy of the final days of New Pop. But it was the packaging and style of rebellion that mattered: the medium not the message. 'Relax' achieved notoriety, and world sales, after BBC Radio 1 disc jockey Mike Read listened to the lyrics a little too closely causing the corporation to censor its transmission, but all Frankie had to do was 'relax' and the rest came: money and fame and law-suits. Advertising's use of the song in later years effectively neutered any significance 'Relax' had left for the field of sexual politics, and the images of the 'Two Tribes' video became 'real' when Reagan and Gorbachev met for the world's press in Moscow.

This state of what Jean Baudrillard, as well as more cautious semioticians like Umberto Eco, have termed 'hyperreality' – where according to Baudrillard the 'real' seems to *follow* the image, where the image 'appropriates reality for its own ends, when it anticipates it to the point that the real no longer has time to be produced as such'[7] – is crucial for understanding the formations of Political Pop and Post-Political Pop. However, whereas, a theorist like Baudrillard refuses to periodise 'hyperreality', or particular shifts within it, the change in modalities represented by Frankie and Bruce Springsteen suggest that in the years around 1983-4 this state of affairs took on a new dimension: New Pop became Political Pop.

The underpinning philosophy of this new formation of Political Pop was, as we have argued, essentially a folk ideology. If anything disturbed the complacency of mainstream rock and pop definitions in the 1980s, it was the re-discovery and re-invention of 'world' or 'global' music: a kind of folk revival for the late twentieth century. From the flamenco of Ketama and Gypsy Kings, the East European folk music of Les Mystere Des Voix Bulgares, Balkana and Marta Sebestyen, through multiple African traditions, Bhangra to English country dance, the range of music bracketed together has been extremely wide. But what was new about it was its categorisation not its sudden emergence after the era of New Pop. What is now referred to as world, global – or 'roots' – music has a history of descent just like any other popular music form. It is the ambivalent entry of such musical texts and practices into pop and rock music discourse as a whole, particularly their recombination within what has been conceptualised as the 'national-popular',[8] which remains important. Although Antonio Gramsci saw the idea of 'national-popular' as progressive, world and roots music has more properly been defined in terms of national *versus* popular, exposing the limitations of theories which analyse popular culture only to ignore, or play down, the racial and social connotations of a specific culture and people – for instance, British or English.

The issues which the reception, and potential incorporation, of 'world music' into music industry categories have raised are most significant in the fields of pop nationalism and internationalism. At the same time as global markets for popular music commodities are being so rapidly expanded, ethnic sounds of such territories (country, reggae, salsa, mbira, rai) pose contradictory and complex problems. There are three main questions which then arise: to what extent should we see these forms as *reflecting* the peoples, communities, cultures of regions and localities? In what sense, if any, can they seriously be seen as oppositional, radical or deviant forms? And how do they help us to map anew the changing shape of the social field of pop music culture so we can better understand how it is regulated, policed and disciplined?

The popularity of country and folk 'roots' forms with audiences and musicians who once embraced a punk ethic and style is indicative of traces of, and responses to, the internationalisation of pop styles over the last decade, reflecting certain sorts of musical forms, especially soul-influenced styles, and particular kinds of production techniques. Such globalisation of pop raises the questions which go to the heart of the cultural politics of world or roots music; what images of America are bound up in these forms and what, precisely, is the significance of other, subordinate, regional and national (especially post-imperialist Britain, and the 'new' post-Cold War Europe) feeling of ambiguity towards what 'the USA' now means in popular cultural forms like rock and pop? Consequently, the concern is with concepts of 'Otherness' in imperialist, colonial and racial themes, and the focus falls on the way in which popular music both articulates and obscures alienation, exclusion and exile. The Mekons are the best example of these themes. From the Fast Product single 'Never in a Riot', recorded in 1977 and released in 1978 when punk was beginning to wane, through numerous country and 'garage folk' renditions, the various mutations of The Mekons prefigured the wider vogue for post-punk 'play' with musical forms which were previously associated with tradition and community. The language and assumptions of community, as well as authenticity and origins, are deeply embedded in the way folk ideology works. The communities involved may be audiences, or classes, or supporters of a cause or nation, but however they differ in form, such communities are somehow a component of the musical rhetoric. Whereas country music usually uses community to defend against, and exclude, outside intrusion and unwanted change, protest music, on the other hand, uses community to evoke the supposed power of people to change their predicament. What is striking about The Mekons is the way that they mix these approaches. Their songs refuse the notion of a pre-existing community, an audience or people with readily identifiable mutually supportive interests. In the wake of the British government's overwhelming defeat of the National Union of Mineworkers in the 1984-5 coal strike there was no more chilling music than The Mekons albums, *Fear and Whiskey* and *The Edge of the World* with their shambolic and rambling treatments of folk and country styles, driven on by their own manic punk history and the sight of the labour movement and its community falling apart under the Thatcherite onslaught. Their own personal, artistic and political resolution was conveyed, perversely, in the bleak darkness of the lyrics wedded to mangled folk and country traditions. As The Mekons ironically proclaim live, '*this* is the folk-rock revival.'

Folk for folk's sake

In Britain the period of the mid-late 1980s witnessed a wave of enthusiasm – once again – for folk forms and ideologies. The 'new folk' passion came from diverse sources; reviewers, the music industry and audiences. A folk revival had already occurred on at least two occasions during earlier parts of the century so critics justifiably queried the labelling of another rock and pop culture fad in such terms. But there are significant features of this tendency – to move *back* to folk, away from the purest forms of rock ideology – which may be of more lasting consequence in cultural politics than yesterday's model on the pop treadmill. As *Folk Roots* editor, folk and blues musician Ian A. Anderson, has pointed out 'younger artists and groups (and quite a few not so young ones) in Britain and elsewhere are increasingly turning to *roots* influences from home and abroad on the less trivial fringes of commercial music.[9] Formerly published as *Southern Rag*, *Folk Roots* in the wake of its name change and glossy design format, increased its sales to around ten thousand a month, symbolising the upsurge in interest in roots/folk music. Anderson's notion of 'folk' is set in terms of 'authentic' folk as opposed to 'commercial pop'. Folk for him is 'non-commercial musics', consumed by 'people who aren't willing to be spoon-fed something that the music biz has concocted as a commodity; dare I say it ... a more *intelligent* audience who will pick up on the integrity of music that comes straight from the heart'.[10] This 'new folk', or to avoid its derogatory connotations, 'roots' sensibility displays some differences from its predecessors. It is wide ranging, encompassing the protest songs of Dick Gaughan and Christy Moore, the ethnic music of Third World countries, as well as the 'Brechtian' folk of the Band of Holy Joy. It differs from folk movements in the 1960s which were essentially pre-feminist in that songs about personal, 'private' life are now sensed as just as political as songs about 'traditional' solidarity in mining and other communities engaged in industrial struggles against pit and works closures. The clash of such differing ideologies, which raise, especially, issues of women being domesticated *and* resisting domesticity, has forced female and male musicians to confront the limits of folk forms and conventions.

Billy Bragg, for many representing the stereotype of Political Pop, for example, released an EP 'Between the Wars' during the coal dispute of 1984-5 dedicated to the work of the Miners' Wives Support Groups. This included Leon Rosselson's 'World Turned Upside Down' and an adapted version of Florence Reece's 'Which Side Are You On ' as well as a title track, written by Bragg, which specifically addressed the audience in celebration of the male manual worker ('miner', 'docker') of Labourism past. The record was commercially successful in Britain, bringing Bragg to a new 'pop' public, but it stands in some contrast to his subsequent material which expressed doubt about personal relationships as well as what he saw as the (a)moral values dominant in 'late capitalism' and de-industrialisation. These later songs cross over to a pop style which allows less certainty about the modern world than the protest songs of working class solidarity. On his 'Walk Away Renee, version' (with Johnny Marr on acoustic guitar, picking out the old Four Tops melody) on another commercially successful EP 'Levi Stubbs Tears', and on the *Talking with the Taxman about Poetry* album, there appeared a self-deprecating humour and an oppenness about the problems of sexual politics which was missing from his earlier punk thrashes on *Life's a riot with Spy vs Spy*. As Bragg wryly admitted in the anguished confrontation with sexual politics on 'Greetings To The New Brunette' from 'the difficult third album' (again with Marr's aid) 'Shirley, your sexual politics have left me all of a muddle.'

The male notion of 'the people' in folk, and the patriarchal values that it enshrines, was undercut here by the pop context and form. When Bragg addressed 'private' concerns his musical ideas were integrated more successfully with his lyrical power. Such folk protest styles have indeed been widely used by, particularly, feminist female singers. A glance through the Womens Revolution Per Minute (WRPM) catalogue in any of the last few years confirms its prominence during the 1970s and early 1980s when it had been unfashionable elsewhere in pop. However, 'post-punk' folksingers, like Michelle Shocked or Phranc (self-styled as a 'Jewish, lesbian feminist' folksinger), have been able to use the pop rather than folk medium to make, respectively, feminist and lesbian commitments, reflecting a self-conscious move out of the commercial ghetto of 'women's music' as it has traditionally been found in the folk music of singers like Holly Near and Meg Christian. In a slightly different vein, the same is true of the gospel and acapella singing of Sweet Honey in the Rock. The radically differing female voices of Bjorg of Icelandic band The Sugarcubes, Kristin Hersch of Boston's Throwing Muses, and Syd Straw of The Golden Palominos perform a similar function in the rock field. Natalie Merchant of 10,000 Maniacs has transformed a discredited female vocal style which was associated with 1970s singer-songwriters like Carly Simon into a vehicle for expressing thoughtful rock humanism.

The politics of the new folk has been most frequently expressed in the classic form of protest. Conventionally, this dissent is an explicit statement of grievance or complaint, or alternatively it is a call to arms. Folk protest had already once before experienced a gradual incorporation into the language of rock. Through the late 1960s and into the 1970s, under the influence of Bob Dylan, protest music, and folk protest in particular, faded from view. Or, rather, the protest was personalised. It came to express only the perspective of the performer, albeit validated by the conventions of folk's populism. These contending positions still vied with each other in the more recent versions of folk ideology. There was most obviously, as was discussed in Chapter 1, the revival of conventional protest music. Singers like

Billy Bragg and Rory McLeod, following the path set by Leon Rosselson and Dick Gaughan, wrote songs which offered explicit political injunctions and judgements, as well as reviving the careers of the older musicians themselves – for instance, Bragg, Rosselson and Gaughan were all prominently involved in live and recorded material which protested at the British government prosecution of the miners strike and Bragg and Rosselson teamed up with The Oyster Band to record 'Ballad of a Spycatcher' satirising the government's handling of the publication of Peter Wright's *Spycatcher* book written about the 'excesses' of the Security Services. The protest in this case was typically couched in the musical idiom of folk. Even when Billy Bragg used an electric guitar for his protests, The Clash stridency in his earlier punk style was soon replaced by a folk picking method. For the interplay of folk sounds and protest sentiments in general, groups like The Proclaimers and The Pogues are the best illustration. The Pogues' mixture of punk and traditional music, rock songs and narrative verse contained strong elements of protest. The sounds of nationalism, evoking notions of common identity, were tied to stories of collective suffering, most obviously in songs about World War I. The protest became shrouded in a heady concoction of raucous good times (embellished later by latin rhythms) and maudlin sentimentality, conjuring images of smoke-filled pubs. Their complaints echoed the jolly protest of music hall and popular song. Just as The Pogues promoted a vision of Irish nationalism, The Proclaimers made similar claims for Scottish nationalism through a combination of Buddy Holly, the Everly Brothers and skiffle and folk styles. Their explicit identification was with local and regional pride in a nation under siege – from without by the government of 'England' under Margaret Thatcher. Their reaction to 'internal' exile at home was to conjure titles like 'The Joyful Kilmarnock Blues' and, in 'Throw the R Away', direct lyrics such as 'You say that if I want to get ahead, The language I use should be left for dead.'

To some extent, music journalist Dave Rimmer captured a pop mood in a phrase when he entitled his history of Boy George and Culture Club and the rest of the New Pop, *Like Punk Never Happened*. After the demise of New Pop, guitar bands, protest singers, festivals and wandering 'hippies' were all more visible (that is in the mass media) aspects of pop music culture. Singer-songwriters in particular have been back in fashion since the mid-1980s. Bob Dylan, the father of all post-1950s versions, played half his set on the 1984 European tour as a solo artist re-interpreting his old songs for his 1980s audience, releasing a live album *Real Live* as a memento. Elvis Costello, too, toured without The Attractions in this period to critical acclaim as the one man bandwagon started to roll, and has continued to play at folk festivals and more off beat venues. Loudon Wainwright III found belated British acclaim as a television show guest on a weekly Saturday night programme hosted by comedian Jasper Carrott. Jackson Browne and Joni Mitchell resurrected their careers with determinedly protest, or socially conscious, 'caring' pop and rock songs. Richard Thompson, perhaps the most unsung of this genre in Britain over the last twenty years, saw a 1970s song 'Withered and Died' recorded by Costello as the B side of his Imposter single 'Peace in Our Time', and meanwhile recorded a solo acoustic album of live songs. After the much publicised divorce with his wife Linda, American rock fame was finally achieved. Thompson himself has always stood outside folk and rock categories, confounding the imposition of pop labels, and his relationship to Political Pop as a social formation is even more tenuous than Dylan, Costello or Bragg. That, however, is not to argue that his work is apolitical; as Robin Denselow claimed in 1975 'there may be no directly socialist overtones to Richard Thompson's work, but he has done as much for English writing as the famous Radio Ballads.'[11]

Thompson's involvement in contemporary music has been perverse. Whilst almost single-handedly changing a conception of what folk music can mean, reworking the relationships between traditional and contemporary forms, he has flirted with more avant-garde approaches (such as on the *Live Love Larf and Loaf* album collaboration with Fred Frith and others) and rock 'muso' gatherings like Anton Fier's Golden Palominos. To some extent, his career pattern has been a result of deliberate policy of courting obscurity (it has been a 'veer', rather than a career, as he has argued in interview[12]) but it signposted many of the more general changes in pop and rock culture in these years, especially around world music. Whilst Thompson's music is now less often labelled as folk, it clearly drew heavily on its roots in Celtic music, as well as rock, and also on Middle Eastern styles. It has, further, plundered English music of several centuries. In 1981 the album *Strict Tempo* (released on the Elixir label and made cheaply for £750 with Dave Mattacks on drums) was a showcase for various traditional and jazz forms well before they became fashionable again. As a role model for the younger vanguard of musicians, though, it was as both a songwriter and guitarist that he was revered. Peter Buck, guitarist with REM, has insisted 'I've been listening to Richard Thompson since I was a kid and he's probably the best songwriter of the last fifteen years ... He reaches to the heart without being maudlin or excessive. What the hell, he's fuckin' great.' Johnny Marr remembers, too, how 'when I was able to start putting chords together I was turned on to Bert Jansch, Pentangle and Richard Thompson and, because of him, to Jerry Donahue'. However, audiences are frequently less reverential than the musicians they listen to. As Simon Frith has recalled[13] at a joint London concert in 1985 with the Boothill Foot Tappers and the Pogues, Pogues fans chanted, soccer style 'Richard Thompson! Richard Thompson! Who the Fuckin Hell is he?' to torment the older Thompson fans. Despite the presence of a Thompson folk contemporary, former Steeleye Span member Terry Woods in The Pogues line-up by the time of the 'Poguetry in Motion' EP, and a single recorded with the Dubliners, The Pogues maintained a 'punkish' disregard for such older, folk influences. The Men They Coudn't Hang, on the other hand – along with The Pogues touted in the music press in these years as the leading lights of punk/folk – displayed a greater affinity with the the contemporary folk music inheritance itself, despite their 'stomp'. The Pogues themselves had extinguished most of their punk musical heritage by time of the release of the 1989 album *Peace and Love*.

Bob Dylan's influence, perversely, was more pervasive. Whilst his own material since, at least, the late 1970s (when he experienced his much-confessed conversion to born again Christianity) is widely regarded as deeply sub-standard, direct homage to his work is paid in pop styles as diverse as Phranc's rifling of his back catalogue to rework 'The Lonesome Death of Hattie Carroll', The Flatmates' recording of 'If Not For You', and the generalised 'theft' of different periods of his output by performers as diverse as Andy White and Felt. Former Plimsoul band member Peter Case, using Dylan sidemen adeptly, symbolised a move in pop thinking in the 1980s by giving up 'new wave' pop to play – to use his term - 'postmodern', self-absorbed solo guitar performances. Organ, bass, drums, guitar rock line-ups have been drawn increasingly to where Dylan left off in the mid-1960s after the albums *Highway 61 Revisited* and *Blonde on Blonde* were recorded. Martin Stephenson and the Daintees' first album paid overt respect to Dylan and to Leonard Cohen, paving the way for Cohen's self-parody and black humour on an album which signalled his own profitable, re-emergence in the late 1980s. On the second Martin

Stephenson LP *Gladsome Humour and Blue* which was marketed with a free poetry book, this took on a straightforward impersonation of the troubadour style. However, Stephenson's live solo performances exhibited a reticence and shyness markedly at odds with the public persona of many 1960s and 1970s male performers, suggesting a different kind of exploration of the fragility and instability of pop's often unitary masculine identities. His Kitchenware label colleagues, Prefab Sprout, explored similar territory – though with a much wider definition of singer-songwriter which included Gershwin and Rodgers and Hammerstein. As singer Paddy McAloon's 'contribution to urban blues' on 'Cruel' from the debut LP *Swoon* in 1984 preciously put it 'I'm a liberal guy, Too cool for the macho ache'. McAloon also explicitly deconstructed the masculine rock myths in later work like 'Cars and Girls', a song directed at Bruce Springsteen above all. In sharp contrast, folk and country performers who had originally emerged in these eras – such as Texans Townes Van Zandt, Terry Allen and Butch Hancock – were able to continue singing traditional masculine songs of hobo hardship. At the same time, female singer-songwriters like Tracy Chapman and Suzanne Vega emerged from the East coast coffee house scene as if it was 1963 again. In England the Rhythm Sisters could rework folk and blues myths for downtown Leeds. It was little wonder, then, that a *Folk Roots* editorial in August 1986 could assert: 'take a wider look and I think you'll find that the situation for live folk and roots music is the healthiest for two decades'.[14] The way that this was commercialised on a global scale, though, was best signified by the rehabilitation of Paul Simon's show business life, which shows a much more complicated picture than *Folk Roots* envisaged. Simon's recording of South African musicians inside South Africa was double edged; it manifestly contravened the cultural boycott, but also gave worldwide publicity to performers like Ladysmith Black Mambazo, paving the way for the world and roots sales and tours bonanza of the late 1980s.

'Folk', in these years, had also come to represent a 'do-it-yourself' ethic, reminiscent of some aspects of punk. Live performances themselves became worthy of note in the music video age. Folk as musical style became less important here than signifying somewhere cheap and easy to play. In a sense, Michelle Shocked and Ted Hawkins simply carried on with the busking and festival hopping which dominated their lifestyles prior to being discovered. Hawkins, especially, has injected this into his style – live performances being conducted sitting atop a crate or stool, glove on one hand, with contrived song fade-outs just as in his Venice Beach days. The music of many such singers cuts across various musical forms (pop, blues, soul, country, folk). They are united only in taking such busking styles to larger and more sympathetic audiences than those in the underground stations of the urban metropolis, or the traffic-free plazas of city centres. 'Have guitar and voice, will travel' is the only ticket necessary. Hawkins, like S.E. Rogie, was brought to a wider public by the singular energies of Radio 1 disc jockey Andy Kershaw. He sang versions of John Denver's 'Country Roads' and 'Green Green Grass of Home', a 1960s hit for Tom Jones, without a trace of postmodern pastiche. The slate, instead, was simply wiped clean in a plain post-apocalyptic folk. Hawkins came over like a twentieth-century Kaspar Hauser, as if he had just managed to scramble out of the bunker to witness a crazy, post-nuclear world without any pop culture signs to guide him except a few battered 45's. Rogie's 1960s Palm Wine Guitar music had a similar 'innocent', unknowing charm.

As, Clive Gregson, one English exponent of this modern mode argues 'the so-called trend towards folk is more a matter of economics. If there's no money to be made in touring you might as well go out with the fewest possible overheads.'[15] Gregson adopted this strategy when his former 1970s and early 1980s pop band, Any Trouble, folded. He set out to practise, for virtually no fee, in the folk clubs he had first played in his formative days; such venues proved an attractive prelude to a work on a solo LP. He stressed, too, that this oblique critique of folk music, the folk revival and folk clubs was shared by many others who frequented them, including his sometime band leader, Richard Thompson. The narrowness of the 'British folkie' ideal, restricting cross fertilisation of some musical forms and traditions, was a particular target of Thompson, who explicitly claimed that:

> The Folk scene needs changing – I'm trying to bring about a revolution. . . it's a matter of organisation, in the sense that Folk clubs are dying on their feet, what you need is to professionalise say 20 folk clubs in Britain. Give them excellent p.a. systems, good seating, improve the decor, and make it a circuit where you can put on really good people and ensure that they get paid real money. You need to create something in between the standard sized 'Rock' gig and the Folk club, you've got to find a middle stage because too many good people get neglected, too many people get labelled jazz and ignored. What you want is a place where jazz, folk, left of field rock etc can all be staged in one venue . . . a circuit of clubs.[16]

Certainly, there were continuities with punk's pub rock connections in the development of the 'new folk'. There was a similar ethos of opposition to stadium rock and the megabuck pop values which became associated with playing in such venues.

One more example of punk's meaning being taken up by the new folk is, in addition to live performance, the area of production. Against a formidable, hi-tech, multi-million dollar industry norm, the recording of a singer like Michelle Shocked on a Sony portable in the middle of a Texan field with only the crickets and passing trucks for company was an about turn. Pete Lawrence made the recording as an initial development for his own label, Cooking Vinyl, which was formed in 1986 after Making Waves, another small, independent 'roots' business which employed him, went into bankruptcy. The triumph of the *Texas Campfire Tapes* LP in the independent charts helped the label establish itself as an important element in the new folk, punk/folk, world and roots markets. Ry Cooder's pioneeering archival efforts in the 1970s and early 1980s, which gave publicity to the talents of musicians like accordian player Flaco Jimenez for example, were an inspiration for the resurfacing of world music in pop tastes, though not necessarily reflected in his own record sales. Pete Lawrence[17] justifies Cooking Vinyl's commercial concentration on, and redefinition of, world and roots music, partly on the loyalty of live audiences at Cooder's concerts in Britain since the 1970s. Despite some critical disdain for *The Slide Area* album released in 1982, Cooder played eight consecutive nights at London's Hammersmith Odeon as part of a European tour in that year, and Lawrence cites such audience figures as partly justifying a small label venture into the musical field which Cooder was uncovering several years earlier with albums like *Show Time* and *Chicken Skin Music*. Cooder's subsequent work had been focused around film theme music. Following the former critical successes of *The Long Riders* and *The Border* movies, his part in the eerie soundtrack for Wim Wenders' *Paris, Texas* became his major claim to imternational notoriety rather than as a mass-market seller of recordings by his own band. Significantly, too, it is as a rock slide guitar session player – on 1960s 'underground' classics such as Captain Beefheart and the Magic Band, *Safe as Milk* album – and smoothly imitated in the late 1980s by bands like Scottish group Texas, that Cooder remains revered in rock music culture. In 1983 BBC Radio 1 included him in their features on 'Guitar Greats' along with James Burton, Jimmy Page, Eric Clapton, Pete Townshend and Jeff

Beck.[18] In that sense, roots' fashionability is more a register of shifts in the production and distribution of commodities in the music industry than a particularly new audience sensibility. Moreover, the way in which 'folk' do-it-yourself values have become most widespread in the international pop industry is through the relatively cheap and accessible new technologies – such as the Roland 808 drum machine – dominating the burgeoning underground dance music scene. Recordings made in Manchester council flats in Hulme became as significant as those from hi-tech studios in New York as the decade drew to a close because of the general improvement in the quality of electronic technologies for recording and making a whole variety of popular music.

One more significant factor in the folk/roots/world categorisation, though, is a reverence for the musical forms involved, or musicianship itself. Los Lobos, for instance, were able to claim a long apprenticeship of playing cheaply and enthusiastically to a rapidly growing Spanish-speaking immigrant population in the United States of America, before their eventual chart breakthrough as a result of association with, initially Paul Simon, and, subsequently, *La Bamba*, the film version of Richie Valens' life story. Their widely admired technical competence and commitment to authenticity with traditional instrumentation helped to solidify their reputation despite commercial recognition. There were strands in 1980s pop, nevertheless, which have found the folk attitude and ideologies involved a matter for pastiche and parody, a means of following, rather than denying, the post-punk lineage. Playing with the musical and political signs of folk, and in particular the 1960s infusion of folk into rock ideology, has for some contemporary musicians been a carefully worked-out practice. Bands like the Jesus and Mary Chain, especially on their first album, *Psychocandy*, released in 1985, had pastiche off to a t. Arch ironicists in pop archive terms, they plundered the familiar back catalogue territory of the Byrds, Velvet Underground, Jan and Dean, and the Beach Boys, but soaked it in white noise and carefully sculpted feedback. Psychedelia in its original incarnation in the 1960s counterculture signified a set of lifestyles based around drug use which no longer pertain. As Marek Kohn points out in his book 'on heroin', a single by the band at this stage of its development was a perfect instance of postmodern pastiche; the 'record in question, "Some Candy Talking" by the Jesus and Mary Chain (Blanco Y Negro) seemed to be attempting a pastiche of the old veiled drug allusions popular in the "underground"music of a bygone era. Lines like "give me more of that stuff" set up such an effect with a bare minimum of subtlety.'[19] There are similar properties embedded in the music of many of the bands in the wave of (mainly) white 'indie-pop' which had mushroomed in Britain by the mid-1980s, and which the Jesus and Mary Chain rode with characteristic panache, turning their backs on their audience in performance, resisting pop conventions and norms of entertainment and consumption. Bands who contributed to the much-vaunted C86 tape (later a vinyl album) compiled by the *New Musical Express* in 1986 were less a 'new wave', a new deviant 'punk' subculture devoted to the independent sector of the record industry and explicitly politicised against the Thatcherite entrerprise culture, than a new class of pop archaeologists. The Jesus and Mary Chain's dedication to reworking 1960s bands – as well as 1970s influences like Tom Verlaine's group Television – were mirrored by other bands' capacity for quotation, plunder and manic referencing of the twists and turns of pop history.

The Bodines, Pastels and Primal Scream's pastiche of the 'classic' pop single from Beatles/Rolling Stones/Kinks mid-1960s era, or 1970s New Wave, or early 1980s New Pop bands like Nick Heyward's Haircut One Hundred are, it could be argued, distinct from parody. For literary theorist, Fredric Jameson, pastiche is a kind of 'blank parody', a take-off of an earlier form which itself no longer exists. In Jameson's argument[20] such an aesthetic is everywhere amongst postmodern texts. For him, The Beatles' and Rolling Stones' 1960s singles represented a stage of 'modernism', or even 'high modernism' in pop history, predictably leading him to conclude that 'postmodernism' in pop in the 1980s was a regressive departure. Jameson's view, though, is overly pessimistic; and particularly his criticism of those who employ pastiche for their *refusal* to innovate stylistically. What the 'perfect pop' of these and other bands produced was a 'critical deconstruction' of the rock tradition – of rock theory, of a rock aesthetic – without involving a simple return to its 'origins'; it cannot be read as a revival, pure and simple of earlier moments in pop history. Further, the 'refusal' involved is, as we shall see in Chapter 4, of a rather different nature.

There are also other aesthetic implications invoked in the sampling (both through new sampling technology and skilful musicianship) of the past history of pop and rock music culture, which go beyond the desire to create a pastiche of a certain point in the individual or collective pop memory. Many of the young musicians involved in these archaeological digs have, literally, excavated their older brothers' or sisters' – or friends – record and tape collections. These were the sounds they grew up with, half-heard through open bedroom doors or blasting out of the radio on revivalist music programmes, even though they were too young to have experienced the impact of the music first hand. That Petrol Emotion, for instance, had band members who were originally with Feargal Sharkey in the Irish punk group, The Undertones, and who stressed that their 1980s fascination with the music of 1960s and early 1970s bands like Captain Beefheart and the Magic Band was no coincidence. The records which influenced them at home in Northern Ireland in the mid-1970s were from precisely those sources, even though what they ended up playing to become a household 'punk' name on Top of the Pops was a mixture of three-chord thrash mixed with easily memorable songs of teenage pleasure and pain. More pertinently, the same band members testify to the special place in both eras (mid-1970s and mid-1980s) of their professional lives of records like the *Nuggets* collection of 1960s punk and garage classics released in the early 1970s on Elektra following archive work by Lenny Kaye. Kaye's own influence on the 'grain' of popular music in the last twenty years is not inconsiderable. As well as being guitarist in the underrated Patti Smith group in the punk era, his production credits have included Suzanne Vega's debut LP and James' first album – though injecting a much weaker feel than the band's tough 'live' sound would have demanded – and he played a general part in the resuscitation of New York's avant-rock bohemia (John Zorn, Sonic Youth and so on) in the 1980s.

The musical legacy of punk itself is also much more complicated than is often claimed. At the very least, the transmission and dissemination of musical styles of that era to the next is only now becoming clearer. In one pop lineage there is a continuity between the 'classic' pop singles of the mid-1960s, punk in the 1970s, New Wave in the late 1970s and jangling 'indie-pop' in the mid-1980s. As Clive Gregson puts it in talking about influences on Any Trouble, in the punk era 'there were good pop bands around if you listened – Buzzcocks for instance'.[21] Any Trouble's own style came directly from those New Wave pop bands like Elvis Costello and the Attractions, and Squeeze, and the influential producer John Wood. The Soup Dragons, Razorcuts and other 'indie' bands fit neatly into the Pete Shelley and Buzzcocks file: musically, the Sex Pistols were always essentially a 'bad' rock band despite their impact on cultural politics of the mid-late 1970s, as borne out by John Lydon's eventual collaboration in PIL's 1986 single 'Rise' with the former Cream drummer, Ginger Baker. 'Indie' bands like the Shop Assistants and (We've Got A) Fuzzbox (and We're Gonna Use It), in their initial stage, at least, before they found mainstream chart success with 'glam' send-ups, were significant not just for the near exclusivity of female members (playing instruments, not merely as vocalists) but also for their combination of elements of 1960s folk-rock with 1970s punk to produce music which was contrived to seem spontaneous, uncommercial and subversive. They did not rework folk conventions so much as borrow the ethos.

Whatever may be thought of these developments, whether or not they are seen as confused – and confusing – parts of folk history, it is clear that the concept of 'folk' remains a potent emblem in pop and rock iconography. It stands for the ways in which music is made and judged, for the way it is understood and decoded. It is more than sounds and styles. It is this renewed folk ideology – in the sense of a particular mode of producing and consuming music – which has supplanted the dominant notion in the New Pop era. In that formation the politics was based on a 'pop critique' (irony, plasticity, and so on) continuing yet another phase of art ideology and its inroads into pop.[22] In the 1980s social formation of Political Pop, 'art ideology' does not disappear, but the terrain changes. Folk ideology, which fed rock and pop music culture in the mid-late 1980s with a series of arguments over key terms, such as community, authenticity, integrity, roots, and truth, became the dominant basis for 'politicisation' of pop. As Simon Frith has argued the 'protest music of the 1960s sprang from the USA's folk community' which was 'an ideological community, bound by its attitude to music-making itself'.[23] It is this folk ideology, with its emphasis on 'songs and lyrics, on honesty and commitment', on the lack of 'separation of performer and listener' which is being returned to, revisited, and revived in the recent hegemony of Political Pop. Though punk's art school connections were of overriding importance, the *belief* in punk as a popular, people's folk music which would reverse the taint and 'corruption' of rock's commercial orientation in the late 1960s and early 1970s remains. It is precisely such conviction which is the mainstay of the phenomenal popular worldwide success of a band like U2; the fact that U2's own musical trajectory was from punk in the late 1970s to the reworking of ethnic

American folk and blues styles on the best selling albums, *The Joshua Tree* and *Rattle and Hum*, simply serves to underscore this continuity of ideology.

'White ethnicity' was how Dick Hebdige[24] described punk in the late 1970s, but the search for musical 'roots' – both black and white, personal and political – has been considerably more complex than such an epithet may imply. Punk ideology certainly addressed problems of tradition, ethnicity, and belonging in a cultural formation where sexism, racism and nationalism were beginning to play more significant political roles than at any time since 1945. Political consensus around social democracy was fracturing deeply in 1976-7. Some of punk's most lasting effect on popular memory is due to its capacity to construct a sense of 'loss' of such consensus, particularly the uneasiness which comes when the nature of what is lost is unclear or ambiguously interpreted in the first place. The gender and racial dimensions of this loss are significant, too. A return to a mythical rock culture founded on white male patriarchy is a fundamental feature of some musical forms and associated subcultures in the years after punk – witness, at one level, the massive white masculine popularity of heavy, speed, thrash and death metal from Bon Jovi at one end of the spectrum to Napalm Death at the other. In Dick Hebdige's survey of Caribbean music[25] and cultural identity he muses about his own white roots in the context of an account of young blacks in Britain trying to discover their identities through reggae, hip-hop and rap music. He asks, jokingly, where his own might be found, whether in 'Morris dancing' or 'Baltic sea shanties.' Or it could be added, too, the country forms of American popular music as well as European folk. What is clear from the discussion in this Chapter is that changes in the years since punk have forced the question of the relationship of musical forms to cultural identities on us more sharply since Hebdige's investigations, which were mostly undertaken in the 1970s. The 'times' have become, apparently, more precarious, more characterised by a sense of danger and anxiety which, curiously, make folk dancing and sea shanties more relevant than they may seem at first sight. How folk forms and ideologies help to shape and reconstruct pop desire and passion – in terms of sexuality and gender as well as locality – in this period is the issue which is then brought onto the agenda. How do they connect with the twin developments of the simultaneous 'shrinking' of the postmodern world and the expanding globalisation of the markets for pop consumption?

The edges of the world

Within pop's global village in these (post)modern times, the term global or world music has come to signify a complex development of the roots of Anglo-American popular music. In many corners it is read as a sign of resistance to pop blandness, and as a new form of the 'national-popular': a form of popular art rooted in the specific national tradition of the Gambia, Mali, Cuba, Hungary or Brazil. Manchester's Bop Cassettes, the tape label which promotes global music as a voluntary association so that 'the profits go to the bands instead of the bosses', specifically defines itself against the routine pop process of 'pap product' and 'designer blandness'. In contrast, Bop's ideology starts with 'a musical philosophy, with music that is real, creative and exciting ... Music that is rooted in the lived experience of different cultures; ethnic, jazz, roots and world music ... This is music that people can genuinely enjoy, explore and learn from.' Importantly, a folk ideology permeates every aspect of the music's production. Bop argue for the use of a form 'that is attractive and affordable', which with the exception of an ill-fated venture into 'indie-pop' on the Manchester North of England vinyl album, has seen its evolution as a mainly 'cassette-only label that releases regular runs of well packaged tapes from local and international bands'. Recording, manufacturing and packaging are Bop's responsibility. Bop's links with the Bristol-based organisation WOMAD (World of Music Arts and Dance), which after Peter Gabriel's personal initiatives in the early 1980s became synonymous with the world music form through talking books and festivals, has further helped to develop the institutions producing world, roots or global music in Britain. Various other small record companies – Sterns, Cooking Vinyl, Rogue, Earthworks, Triple Earth, World Circuit, GlobeStyle and Hannibal – have developed a mutual support system which helps to mitigate the control of the majors who dominate the record market (Sony/CBS, WEA, RCA, EMI, Polygram and so on). But despite such good intentions, and musical reworkings of folk forms and ideolgies, as was noted in Chapter 1, there is no 'essence' of opposition in world, roots or global music. Soca, mandinka or mqbanga music are being presented and packaged differently today, but they are not new forms in themselves. Combinations of tradition and modern recording technology, like Ofra Haza's 'three hundred-year-old Yemenite songs and a beat-box', represent new conflicts of cultures which disrupt, for a time, received notions of pop taste but they may be interpreted and used in a variety of ways and in diverse contexts. The meaning of such music is not a given, constant, condition of the musical form. It is inseparable from its context, from its production in a pop world where more and more sounds from a range of regions are needed to fill the gaps in the global airwaves and sonic devices, but where manufacture and marketing are ever more concentrated. It is in this nexus, that the meaning of 'America', 'Europe' and the 'West', becomes crucial.

The cultural terms of the debate about world, global, or 'roots' music have often been set out in the opposition 'authentic folk culture' versus 'commercial pop'.[26] The struggle to resist the commercialisation of the folk culture is, then, what makes the world or global music scene come to claim its resistance or opposition to dominant pop and rock music culture. Rock, too, uses this argument at various times in pop history to disinguish itself from pop. The problem is that these terms are already produced within the pop process, and they are overlaid by other problematic binary distinctions such as First and Third World, or West and East Europe. The 'national-popular' conceptualisation which is used to justify the promotion of world or global music as a resistant or radical subculture runs up against the changes in the commercialisation of pop music culture and the consequent shifts in the notions of national, international and popular. In theorising postmodernism as the dominant cultural logic of what he calls 'late capitalism' Fredric Jameson[27] agrees with a number of other writers that 'postmodernism is strictly a first world phenomenon'. But, as he points out, this, in his view, 'new' cultural imperialism is a way of living time in Third and Second World countries. Moreover, Jameson says that it is 'America' which is being exported and deployed anew:

> It starts with that premise, that it is not only first world but North American, it's American, in the limited sense of the United States, this is something the Europeans, who are also first world, constantly remind us of. This is the first distinctively global North American style, and the Europeans have bits and pieces of it but they don't have the whole thing.
>
> One starts from that general premise, that this is not unconnected to the United States, but just as the U.S. is a first world country that also contains a lot of third world, so also the third world has bits of the first world, that is, social classes or yuppie classes or jetset classes who have a kind of global postmodern culture and who co-exist with all sort of levels of cultural publics, all the way down to pre-capitalist publics in Indian societies and so forth.[28]

The problem, however, is precisely the nature of the 'co-existence' of these cultures, especially given the interpenetration in terms of time and space of the global media, of which pop and rock music culture is a key part. Jameson, in development of his work on postmodern culture and capitalism seems to want to suggest that 'other voices can and do exist outside or in spite of the commodified hyperspace of Ist world postmodernism – even though these other voices apparently can only speak in the 3rd world.'[29] Resistances of the 'Other'- in this case, the folk cultures of the Third World – are thus given a new and revived importance in the politics of the postmodern condition by writers such as Jameson. But the claim relies on a reintroduction, on a new plane, and on a new time scale, of the 'authentic' folk culture versus 'inauthentic' commercial, commodified pop culture distinction. How should this be applied, for instance, to the collaboration between the rock singer Van Morrison and Irish folk band, The Chieftains? Or the 'mixing' of Scottish and Irish music in a folk 'super' band like Relativity? Or the punk and post-punk music of the Welsh 'underground' on labels such as Anhrefn and Ofn? The key in all these cases is not the commodified/uncommodified distinction so much as an identification with the Celtic languages defined against a popular culture suffused with imperialist and colonial rhetoric.

It is plain to see how easily world and global music can come to represent a ready-made, intact 'other' voice which forms a resistance to the total commodification of the First World. Yet this assumes a – false – division between the First and Third, or for that matter Second, Worlds in pop and rock discourse. The hierarchy of centre and periphery, mainstream and margin no longer holds in the cultural politics of pop. Instead, we need to see more clearly how the 'ex-centric' or 'off-centre'[30] can become part of a politics of the 'edges'. As Linda Hutcheon argues in a different context:

> Postmodernism retains, and indeed celebrates, differences ... The modernist concept of single and alienated otherness is challenged by the postmodern questioning of binaries that conceal hierarchies (self/other) . . . Difference suggests multiplicity, heterogenity, plurality, rather than binary opposition and exclusion.[31]

Whilst the danger of taking postmodern plurality in pop and rock music culture at face value needs to be remembered, this is a more optimistic reading of the possibilities of postmodernism than the argument of Fredric Jameson. To be 'ex-centric, on the border or margin, inside yet outside'[32] in the languages and cultures of pop is increasingly difficult, but is made possible by changes in both technology and ideology.

One version of this possibility comes from rock theory and assumes that a 'new underground' – a new bohemia – can be identified on the basis of an 'independent' pop music sector. Following on from the 1960s counter-culture and 1970s punk this argument builds a new utopian pop vision. There is some substance for such a claim, but it is relatively weak nevertheless. An independent label like New Zealand's Flying Nun records, for example, responsible for promoting bands such as The Chills amongst others, was able to maintain its 'DIY spirit which shouldn't be compromised' and at the same time help to re-introduce, with other such labels, a 'distinct freshness and energy' to counter what it saw as the 'blandness which plagued independent music in the UK since the early 1980s.'

But essentially 'independence' no longer signifies 'deviance' in the way that rock theory claims. As Dave Haslam argues:

> knowing what I know about the way the music press works and knowing what I know about how the industry works, perhaps my most sensible response would be to have had nothing to do with them . . . or you say 'I'll break them', or you actually have a bit more of a realistic attitude and I think this is what's been the change in the so-called Underground. It might have something to do with Thatcherism. For instance, how independent do I want to be if the cost of being pure independent is to be marginalised. Do I want to be independent? And if the only way I can intervene is to be assimilated, perhaps I should allow myself to be assimilated, if that's the only way to work. Because you've got to deal with them, and that's the line that the Underground has to take – that you stake your claim, artistically, which you try to do with as great a degree of independence as possible. But once you move out of the office, then you have to got to deal with Thatcher's real world, because otherwise no one's going to hear your records, no one's going to buy your fanzine, and your dream is to be like a little blip and you don't want that to happen. That's my problem, and the way I deal with it, to be honest, is bewilderment, and that's my main feeling about the music industry. Let's see how I can get out what I want – how to survive?[33]

In the next Chapter we shall examine what happened to the much heralded 1980s 'new bohemia', and what the story means for the policing and regulating of pop music culture in the 1990s.

Jim Morrison's tomb, Père Lachaise, Paris. Decay of the 1960s rock generation?

Dancers at the Haçienda, Manchester.

Soul weekenders' reply to the tabloids' image of lager louts.

Happy Mondays, archetypal 'scallies'.

Stone Roses, the 'new' psychedelia with a dance groove.

Smiley culture: British rapper, with heavy male jewellery.

Break-dancing from the early 1980s, a phenomenon which declined as the decade wore on and the participants got more involved in making music.

Smiths lads.

Smiths fans recreate *The Queen is dead* album sleeve shot.

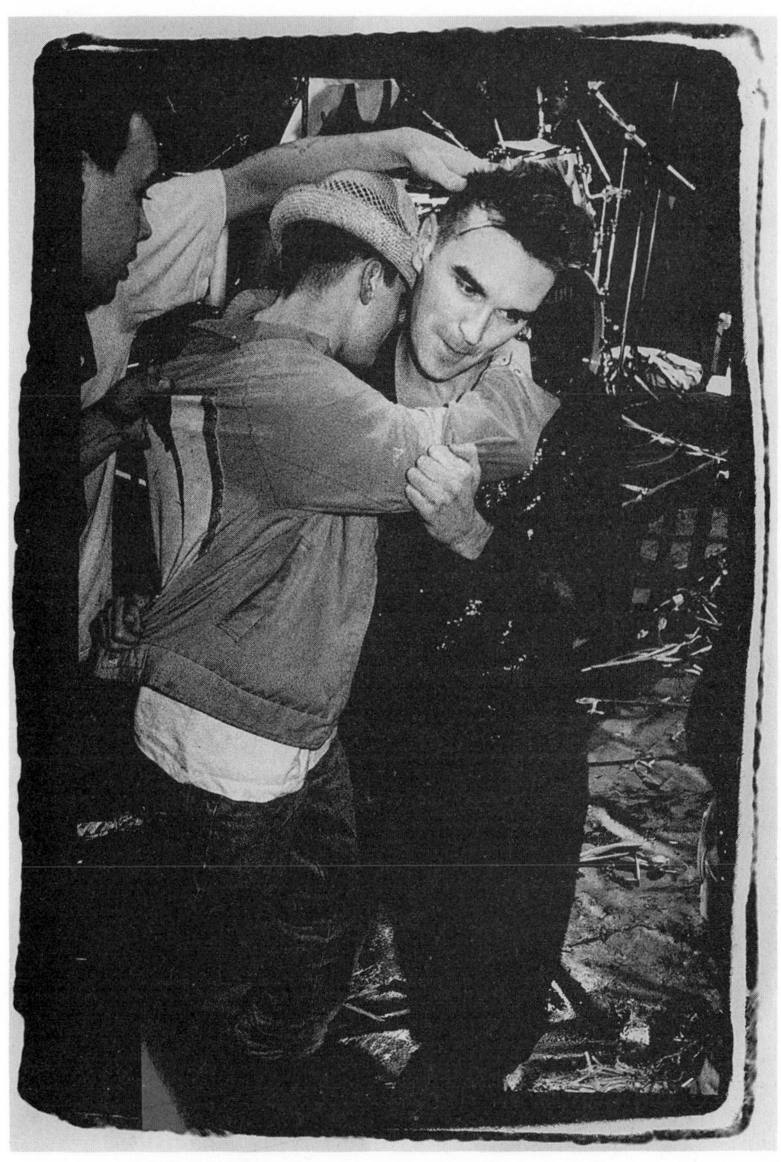

Morrissey and fan at his first solo concert.

Soul weekender, Prestatyn, North Wales – not everything happens in the metropolis!

Public Enemy in militant black power pose.

Clint from Pop Will Eat Itself and Chuck D from Public Enemy model contrasting youth styles.
[*facing*] 'Monsters of Rock' at Castle Donington in the early 1980s.

Todd Terry, New York DJ and ace house producer, hiding behind the smiley image.

4

One nation under a hoof: whatever happened to the new bohemia?

At least since the punk era of the mid-late 1970s, the notion of 'independent' has for better or worse come to signify 'underground', notwithstanding Neighbours' television show star Kylie Minogue's late 1980s successes. Punk, and its aftermath, was a highpoint of the sales, though not necessarily the influence, of independent records in the industry. John Peel, the disc jockey most responsible for promoting independent music in British public service broadcasting over the past twenty years, argues that it is increasingly difficult to pick out good records within the independent sector, as compared to the late 1970s or early 1980s, despite the success of the release of Peel Sessions records on his own Strange Fruit label, a deal wrung out of the BBC after considerable and protracted struggle. For Dave Haslam of Play Hard records 'there is no reason why there shouldn't be space for independent records' but:

> if you look at the sales of independent records over the last ten years, since the great days of independent music as a form then sales have fallen rapidly and considerably. If you were to compare say Play Hard with Factory, then the first thing you would notice would be sales of singles. We probably sell ten per cent of the amount of singles that Factory sold at the same time in their development. A successful single for us is for example King of the Slums' 'Vicious British Boyfriend' which had, when it came out, a feature in NME, a feature in *Melody Maker*, a feature in *Sounds*. There were very enthusisatic singles reviews on the singles reviews pages. They were on Snub TV the day the single came out. John Peel had been playing them for two weeks. Everything was right for them to sell a lot. It sold twice what our distributors said it would sell but it sold a total of seventeen hundred copies which is nothing compared to sales of an independent record ten years ago that had the same kind of media coverage, the same kind of things being said about it. It would probably have sold ten times that amount. That's the reality of an independent label now, the fact that your market is almost non-existent.

I don't mind that. I'm quite happy to work with that. I never believed that any records have a divine right to sell, or to break even, or anything like that. I'm not interested in that. Obviously I care in the long term that the financial future of Play Hard isn't too difficult, but if the records are good and have people saying nice things about them, then that's OK. If the bands are happy, and we treat everyone well, and we don't piss on anyone, then that's alright, that's success. My concern would be that all the people who might like a record have heard it. That's a change that has worked against us - the major labels' control over the airwaves may have something to do with it.

Subcultural theories of pop, youth culture and deviance would predict the continuation of a youth subculture around 'independent' music in the 1980s. This assumption, however, fails to register the fact that independent records have usually reflected the market differentiation and the massive pluralism of pop taste available from the major record companies. For Play Hard, for instance, there has been a 'strength through diversity'. For Dave Haslam this is not necessarily a matter of 'following a trend'. In his experience as a disc jockey, 'there is still a huge amount of tribalism, or style facism.' Specifically, at Play Hard, he says, that:

when we come to mail out the records for promotional purposes we do have to send them in different directions. When an MC Buzz B record comes out we send them to different people than when a King of the Slums record comes out. There is a little bit of a crossover, but again when The Bodines and The Train Set come out we put them in the same box. We have to acknowledge what we are dealing with – a King of the Slums market and an MC Buzz B market which are in themselves unique and we're not able to channel them to any established market. Obviously Buzz B belongs a bit to the hip-hop market but its going against the grain of a lot of hip-hop. And again King of the Slums are too unique to say 'ah, we have the new Wedding Present on our hands.'

The context of such hyper-local initiatives pitted against and within the global development of the cultural industries is extremely important. It raises the question of local and national government intervention, or private alternatives to public investment. Dave Haslam argues, for example, that 'making music is like making cars' and that 'there's no more reason for a left-wing council to subsidise music making than there is for them to subsidise car manufacture. At certain times certain national and local governments have found it necessary to subsidise car making inorder to create jobs. That's fine, if the same is true of music they should step in. But the idea that that would help local culture or be of benefit to the artists I think is wrong.' The question of the independence of the independents in the music industry took on a sharper edge when Red Rhino, the main distributor within The Cartel (distributing independent records) responsible for the North of England, went into liquidation in 1988 leaving debts owing to many of the most hyper-local projects in the industry.

Cultural regeneration of British cities which has become a central part of the Thatcher government's political planning also has important economic implications for notions of independent music, deviance and youth culture in the wake of pop's globalisation during the 1960s, 1970s and 1980s. A quite different concept of youth culture is involved with all elements of opposition and resistant ironed out. John Boyd writing on 'trends in youth culture' in the British Communist Party theoretical monthly, *Marxism Today*, in December 1973 felt confident that the 'label youth culture was probably invented by the IPC publishing monopoly rather than by writers or readers of Marxism Today.' In today's entirely removed political and economic conditions, where youth *cultures* proliferate and Youth Culture is firmly locked into the advertising industry and which demands fresh evaluation of received wisdoms, this formerly orthodox viewpoint – though much discredited – has become persuasive. Furthermore, those subcultural theorists who had taken this argument as fallacious have been forced to re-examine old certainties. Once upon a time, in the late 1970s, Dick Hebdige confidently pronounced that:

> The term 'counter-culture' refers to that amalgam of 'alternative' middle class youth cultures – the hippies, the flower children, the yippies – which grew out of the 60s and came to prominence during the period 1967-70. . . Whereas opposition in subculture is, as we have seen, displaced into symbolic forms of resistance, the revolt of middle-class youth tends to be more articulate, more directly expressed and is, therefore, as far as we are concerned, more easily read.[1]

From the vantage point of more than a decade later it is easier to question such a view. Such standard ways of reading the relations between subcultures, youth culture, pop and deviance in particular social formations dissolved in the 1980s as the fixed identities and meanings of youth styles gave way to a supposed fluidity of postions, poses and desires and a much-hailed (in postmodernist circles) transitory, fleeting adherence to lifestyles – for some theorists, *the* sign of postmodernity. The class and gender stereotypes of the previous two decades were confounded time and time again in the 1980s, and the notion of popular music as a youth cultural form, which has underpinned subcultural theory since its inception, has been severely tested. In particular, punk – which served as the major focus for Hebdige's readings, and in the process considerably post-dated the subcultures and counter-culture written about with his Centre for Contemporary Cultural Studies colleagues – was to leave a more complex legacy. Amongst punk's myriad meanings, the myth of its role as the hippies' revenge, extinguishing the peace and love logo in the process, is least understood. In the era of MTV, the decline of New Pop and the 'death of the soul boy'[2] craving there was opened up a space for experiments with the accepted conventions associated with 'hippy' and 'punk'. Hippy, in this new meta-language, came to mean either those who are old enough to have experienced the 1960s and its rock myths first hand, or alternatively those who nurture a naivety (or in some cases plain dishonesty) in regard to the spiralling commercialisation of the industry. Goth band The Mission, whose music recalled, deliberately and directly, the late 1960s and early 1970s, reflected self-consciously in their long-haired fashion styles and Led Zeppelin and Jimi Hendrix infatuations, argued indignantly that 'alot of people say we're hippies. Well, we're not, we're punks.'[3] Speed metal band, The Electro Hippies, recalled this debate ironically with their album title *The Only Good Punk is a Dead One.*

Contemporary youth styles daily deconstruct the meaning of these moments in the cultural histories embodied in a variety of academic disciplines such as leisure studies, cultural studies, sociology of deviance and criminology. They also reconstruct them in and for the present. What is striking, too, is the way in which certain cultural forms, in particular popular music styles like folk, punk, psychedelia, electro and reggae, have been ripped out of their earlier settings. This new *bricolage* in pop discourse has, of course, a fresh political and economic context and the meanings of disco, latin, soul and funk forms as they circulate and recirculate again and again in the pop process are inextricably bound up with the commodity producing mode of the late twentieth-century popular music industry. But the precise nature of this commodity production is crucial; pop is the best example of what Jean Baudrillard has analysed as hyperreality, a world of self-referential signs. In other words, a world where the signs have become separate from their referents. The diversity of folk ideology, as the basis for Political Pop, which was analysed in Chapter 3 is a case in point: folk as opposed to rock (commerce), folk as opposed to pop (fake), folk (hippy) as opposed to punk/post-punk, and so on. Such potential diversity of meaning is an integral part of the circulation of pop commodities. The same is also true of the much vaunted 'new bohemia'.

Forward to the past?

The analysis of the regulation of pop 'counter-cultures' in this book is underwritten by a pervasive and misleading dichotomy: a 1960s 'oppositional' middle-class youth culture and a 1980s youth consumerism. More than twenty years on from the 1960s 'counter-culture' which Hebdige, and Stuart Hall[4] amongst others, have theorised, there were spotted, by some commentators, new 'alternative' or 'underground' musics and lifestyles. Such a 'new bohemian' figure exists, though, in a global media imagery set in a much colder cultural climate compared to the economic and political conditions which spawned the politics of the first 'Summer of Love' in 1967, and its tortured aftermath in the 1970s. Moreover, its wide dispersal makes it difficult for the mass media to chart. It is in many ways a disparate conglomeration, thrown up as the cultural debris from the dominance of Style Culture in an earlier period. As Jon Savage has noted:

> In the space torn between styles, what interests me is not a 'return to rock' – in America it never went away ... but the chance that there is for the voices that have been excluded by Style Culture's metropolitan bias to make themselves heard. There is a new, uncharted area of youth culture: it might include the Rock fans or Goths that populate any provincial city or small town ... it will also include another group which because it is not organised in consumption, is not deemed worthy of media attention. These days, this means that it might as well not exist. Yet any observer will have noted a large amount of people – disparagingly called 'hippies' – who operate like the *Wandervögel* of the Twenties, moving from town to town, from festival to 'Peace Convoy', outside the bounds of normal society. Any future account of pop culture must include their bohemian wanderings which are a true index of consumerism in crisis.[5]

Such an important argument, however, does not take sufficiently into acount the possibility that there is no longer – because of changes in Pop Time and Space – room for *any* outside, marginal or bohemian youth culture. Instances of such bohemia appear only at specific points of media interest: the 'hippy convoy' annual clashes with police guarding Stonehenge at the time of the summer solstice, for example. It has no unity bound by musical forms – dance music (house, garage, 'rare groove' soul, and hip-hop) is just as likely to be involved as 'gunge' rock or 'noise' – or fashion styles, though the culture of the second-hand market is dominant, plundering the pasts of pop and youth styles. It is a diverse, disconnected formation which takes in independent record shops and distributors, specialist gigs, clubs, all-dayer and all-nighter events and a variety of associated music – electro, reggae, folk, hardcore, punk, soul, metal. It is not, for a number of reasons, as easy to document as previous youth subcultures partly because of its sheer diversity.

Consequently, it has often been played down in the media, and the perception that there has not been, in mass media terms, an oppositional youth politics or politics of rock in Britain since the late 1970s, tended to provoke a sense of frustration in many commentaries. For some, as was seen in Chapter 2, the response was a relatively straightforward cultural pessimism. At the first signs of a new social movement the orthodox response was to compare it, favourably or – more often – unfavourably, with what had been defined as the 'authentic' prototype of the earlier eras. For others, a cultural optimism has reigned, but on similarly shaky grounds to that of the pessimists, recognising a shift in the terrain but not quite being able to make theoretical sense of it with what were formerly seen as useful analytical tools. What makes the arguments about the cultural politics of popular music and youth culture from either of these poles more complicated is the contribution of the marketing strategies of the major corporations in the cultural industries, which have helped to focus on particular periods of pop history with the deliberate intent of creating a boom in the consumption of artefacts of the time; namely records, tapes, videos, compact discs, books, memorabilia. Punk, Acid House and hip-hop have already enjoyed their revivals as well as longer established pop moments. The target audience for such consumption consists of both those who wish to indulge in a nostalgic recollection of their own, heavily mediated, experiences of the times and events and a new, first time audience who were only busy being born when the products were initially available on the market, supporting the notion in postmodern theory which argues that these cultural products are increasingly 'double-coded'.

Granada TV's venture into this multi-media sales pitch (along with EMI) to celebrate the release, originally in June 1967, of The Beatles LP *Sgt Pepper's Lonely Hearts Club Band* on its twentieth anniversary is a pertinent example. In conjunction with the book of the television film by former Beatles publicist, Derek Taylor, It Was Twenty Years Ago Today painted a heavily mythologised 'counter-cultural' context of the album in such a way as to distance the perceived 'progressive' 1960s from the 'conservative' 1980s, implying that a once bohemian impulse had been incorporated and remained an implausible future project.

Part of the reason for this 'nostalgia mode' is simply due to the sociological trends which have coincided with commercial tactics. There are, in the various media and culture industries, a large group of people between thirty and forty-five for whom the moment of the 1960s counter-culture is a significant point in their own personal and generational autobiography. However, the cultural fascination with the 1960s (and for that matter the 1950s or 1970s) cannot be put down only to demographic changes and the economic needs of the music industry, although as the number of young people declines in the 1990s, and pop history rewinds, 'youth' has come to signify both lower *and* upper reaches of age categories, so that the connection between pop and youth is one which covers anyone, say, between 5 and 55. For one cultural critic, Robert Hewison, popular memory of the 1960s is deeply ambiguous. It is not, Hewison argues, that the era was merely 'better', but that:

> The Sixties were good at a number of things, especially at having a good time, and now, when we are having a bad time, we are inclined to read the words 'too much' with a guilty awareness that the rich substance of the Sixties has been dissipated in the Eighties – and that it was in the Seventies that we began to pay the price. Of course, it is much more complicated than that, and at this distance from events there is still confusion about what took place, as well as ambivalence about its significance. This is because people in the Sixties were particularly prone to mixing myth and reality, style and substance, image and fact. The Sixties have themselves passed into myth more quickly than the period that preceded them.[6]

This mythology of the 1960s is now an important site of ideological conflict in a more general political sense. The new puritanism of the 'moral right' (which ranges unevenly and uneasily from figures such as Victoria Gillick and Mary Whitehouse to Margaret Thatcher and Norman Tebbit) blames what it defines as the moral decay of the 1970s and 1980s on the 'permissive' era of the 1960s, whilst some on the left draw strength from ecological, gay and lesbian, peace and feminist politics which were seen to be a 1970s outgrowth of the 1960s whilst still others, such as Jeremy Seabrook, condemn the rapid consumerist destruction in the 1970s and 1980s of earlier traditional working class communities and their politics. Musically, the 1960s are now, as we have seen, a fount of rock tradition.

The precise definition of the 1960s is also contentious. Robert Duncan, in his highly personalised account of the rock era[7], notes that 'in fact, for my money, the seventies *were* the sixties'. More specifically, Robert Shelton, biographer of Bob Dylan, has noted:

> The worst thing about the sixties is not what happened then, but what has happened since it ended. The sixties is not contained in 1960 to 1969. The sixties were really in two decades: it began in '55 and ended in '74. It began with all the incredible recording activity – Chuck Berry's "Maybelline" and all the folks that were being recorded by the early rock people. It ended with the evacuation of Saigon. That's what I call the sixties – twenty years.[8]

In this revised cultural definition of decades, the 1970s might be better seen as beginning where the 1960s finished (in 1974), and culminating ten years later in the mid-1980s. The 1980s as we have signified them in this book stand much more clearly, then, for the 'past in the present/future now', rather than simply a period of historical time. In that sense, for cultural politics, they are only just beginning, and the years focused on in this book are formative of what the years towards 2000, and beyond, may hold, rather than their closure.

Moreover, the changing consumption of commodities is closely bound up with popular memory of the 1960s and 1970s. At the end of the 1970s, Peter York wrote in *Harpers and Queen* that:

> What is certain is that eye-witness accounts differ radically, not only as to what mattered in the sixties, but about what actually happened. But when asked about the sixties there seems to be a qualitative difference in people's responses – they seem to be confused about what really happened (to them) and what the media had said was happening. This kind of conceptualising seems true across the social board. Most people under forty, in describing the sixties, at least defer to the media sixties. My own main sixties memories, however, seem to be about *things* - having them and wanting them ... The reality of the sixties was new money, new technology, *things* – and the choices they implied.[9]

The commodification of the 1960s which occurred in the 1980s underlines York's salient autobiographical point. Additionally, the American music and cultural critic Greil Marcus has pleaded, commenting on the contemporary significance of versions of the song 'What's So Funny 'Bout Peace, Love and Understanding?', both by the writer Nick Lowe and a later version by Elvis Costello 'What's so funny about peace, love and understanding? Now, nothing. For an instant, the search for peace, love and understanding is what life is all about.'[10] Such a view should, though, make us much more wary of 1960s rock myths and folk ideologies which have become so pervasive in the Political Pop of the 1980s. In particular, there is, for a post-punk generation of 'indie-pop' bands – most of whom were not born in the 1960s – a treacherous melange of musical, cultural, and political memory to draw on, recycle and discard. For instance, Stone Roses' fans caused an unexpected boom in the sales of up to 30" flares and 'Woodstock 69' T-shirts as the band's adaptation of psychedelia and jangle-pop to a dance-floor groove stimulated demand in these items, as well as Joe Bloggs clothing in general. What, then, in this light, are the implications of the pop media search for a new moment of bohemian impulse?

The mid-1980s 'shambling'[11] bands are one instance of the media construction of a 'new' youth culture. In one sense, 1986 was remembered in the popular music media in Britain for shambling, whilst 1987 signified hip-hop and 1988 represented Acid House as far as sections of the music press were concerned. Bands from The Smiths, who began in 1982 and broke up in 1987, at one end of the spectrum through the Mighty Lemon Drops to The Mekons, Stump, Bogshed and Big Flame at the other, were labelled by the music press as shambling, a concept born out of 'shambolic' and 'rambling' first coined by John Peel. According to the writers and fanzines who acted as spokespersons for shambling bands, some of them at least could be categorised together for a number of reasons, especially because of their emphasis on the 1960s, childlike innocence and a 'refusal to grow up'. Simon Reynolds, shambling's most articulate and provocative media defender, argued in 1986 that:

> The 'shambling bands' have widely diverging influences – ranging from Sixties garage and psychedelia to the Velvet Underground to the thrash-pop of the Buzzcocks and Ramones to spiky indie-pop circa 1979. But there is a common legacy derived from punk – a hatred of anything hippy (long tracks, virtuosity, complex instrumentation, mysticism, pomp, fusion). This anti-hippie consensus has itself settled into stifling orthodoxy – an insistence on short songs, lo-fi, minimalism, purism and guitars, guitars, guitars.[12]

What was most notable about shambling bands was the search and struggle for new anti-rock conventions – a 'pop critique' – frequently based around a reworking of folk ideology, which would help to make sense of the contradictory emotional responses appropriate to living in the (post)modern world: loss, despair, nostalgia, solidarity as well as innocence and experience. What shambling shared with some other genres in the pop critique of popular music was a sense of the West's cultural and political desolation, particularly the position of post-imperial societies like Britain, and to a lesser extent the United States of America. It also invoked a desire for a return not to a simplistic optimism of the will (in cultural politics, youth culture and so on) but to a mythology of 'innocence' *before* hope was trampled. The exact location, in historical time, of this rainbow's end is manifestly uncertain since popular memory is itself constructed. But it forces a reconsideration of memory of the 1960s and 1970s, displacing in particular the pre-eminence of punk. As Simon Frith put it in March 1986 at the time of punk's tenth anniversary, 'what matters now is not the rise and fall of punk but why the Shop Assistants ... sound like Judy Collins'.[13]

In this sense there is a significance in the the mannered refusal to grow up of the shambing bands, a deliberately constructed style evident in their dress and choice of band names – The Woodentops, The Rosehips, Talulah Gosh. As i-D put it in its 'pop issue' consumer guide to one version of this 'scene':

> Childlike innocence and assumed naivety permeate the Cutie scene – their clothes are asexual, their haircuts are fringes, their colours are pastel. Cuties like Penguin modern classics, sweets, ginger beer, vegetables and anoraks. Heroes include Christopher Robin. . . . Buzzcocks and The Undertones.[14]

However much this reads like a pastiche of subcultural theory of the past two decades, it provides a stark contrast with the world weary seriousness of the experienced, more professional, older bands who have also turned to 1960s musical forms for their 'roots'. Musically, the most typical example of shambling were bands like the Shop Assistants, whose initial releases were put out (like Talulah Gosh) on the small independent label 53rd and 3rd but who graduated to a larger label (Chrysalis-owned Blue Guitar) for their eponymous debut LP. Their vocal style consisted of pre-pubescent girl voice against Ramones buzzsaw guitar noise or Byrds-influenced jangle, pitting an ambiguous childlike female purity with sharp-edged lyrics. On 'I Don't Wanna Be Friends With You' lead vocalist, Alex (who subsequently left the band to join Motorcycle Boy), sang in a style recalling folk-rock female singers Judy Collins and Sandy Denny though at breakneck speed, and emphasising razor sharp lyrics like 'I don't wanna be civilised, You leave me and I'll scratch your eyes out'. The states of innocence and experience that shambling alluded to were highly contrived and cannot be simply read off with the aid of a set of popular musical signposts. Post-punk knowingness and irony are replaced in this genre by a constructed innocence which builds on the previous historical sense – it does not retreat from it as cultural pessimists like Fredric Jameson have argued. However, whether based on pastiche of 1960s pop, or various more experimental forms, shambling manifestly struggled to wriggle free of the easy categorisation of pop discourse, media pigeon-holes and the insatiable media desire for a new 'punk' youth culture.

Post-Man pop

As the chapters of this book have demonstrated, the spread of 'counter-cultures' by the mass media – in various popular musical fields – is connected to the circulation of rock and pop mythologies. It is, though, the way that these mythologies have been deconstructed that is significant, not the revival and reproduction of 'counter-cultural' positions in another context some twenty or thirty years later. In particular, major changes in cultural and sexual politics since the 1960s need to be taken into account. As was seen in Chapter 3, the (post)modern folk revival is not reducible to 'fingers in the ear' and Aran sweaters. Jazz revivals, bringing to prominence players like Courtney Pine, Andy Sheppard and Tommy Smith, are as much to do with dance as the subtleties of the music. Further, 'style' politics and other post-punk issues of production, distribution and consumption of music-related commodities join forces with the pre-punk concerns of the decay of community, the expression and representation of truth, and the political problems of selling out to commercial interests at the expense of musical integrity and close links with the audience. Part of the difficulty, as we noted in Chapter 2, is that what has been debated under the rubric of terms such as style and 'Style Culture' has been more specifically a question of sexual politics and of gender – of the construction of new 'masculinities' and 'femininities' in the light of the deep inroads made by a resurgent moral conservatism in the West, and a fervent fundamentalist religious doctrine in many parts of the world.

It is not only feminist questions which are being addressed anew, specifically against prevailing folk, pop and rock ideologies. Punk's most radical, long-lasting contribution can still, perhaps, be seen to have been as 'culture shock'. It raised, in particular, specific issues of gender and sexuality which the New Pop era went on to explore. It also posed the problem, in terms reminiscent of discourses of 'the body', of a bloated music industry inexorably committed to pumping every last drop out of consumerism, to commodification of everything including itself. The 'health' of the economic performance of the industry was fundamentally queried even while punk itself was helping to revive and prolong that very structure. Further, it fundamentally subverted a moral economy of pop, undermining previous notions of 'authenticity' and 'truth'. Not that punk itself achieved a new authenticity; it was easily incorporated after a few short months and packaged for the pop and youth culture museum.

The shift from New Pop to Political Pop is not to be mistaken for a move from 'Style Culture' to anti-Style Culture. It is more properly seen as a movement within a series of sites: sexual politics of pop, political economy of pop, and politics of youth culture. A shift from 'gender-bending' Boy George to blue-collar US male Bruce Springsteen is not just a description of some changing consumer pop taste in the mid-1980s but also a statement of changing markets and cultural identities. The figures 'New Man' and 'Post-Feminist Woman' have been important traces in advertising discourses since the early 1980s which are more than simply new consumer categories. Further, a 'feminising' of pop production in the 1980s – from the influence, for example, of gay Hi-Nrg music on chart success of performers such as the Pet Shop Boys, Sinitta and many others through the origins of house music in the gay clubs of Chicago to the glam influences of much heavy metal – is part of a more general media process of feminisation of consumption (of 'mass', or popular, culture) as analysed by postmodern theorists such as Andreas Huyssen and Jean Baudrillard. For Baudrillard, the feminisation of pop culture would be a cause for celebration since the masses' refusal, silence or passivity – the supposedly 'feminine' quality – is, potentially, the means of a radical undermining of the media. However, sexual difference is, for Baudrillard, absorbed into the mass, and there is no possibility of the important shifts in pop and gender being theorised from his position.

Similarly, the media identification of various new bohemian lifestyles in the decade since punk is more than a move from dole-queue to art school and back. It represents a complex shaping and reshaping of subject positions within a variety of discourses. The fall-out from the 'death of youth culture' is, in part, to be found in the multi-faceted, locally based, bohemian 'undergrounds', which are themselves heavily influenced and shaped by the global leisure industry of which pop is now structurally so much an integral part. But significantly it manages, through a number of different tactics and strategies, to suggest new passions and desires which are not pre-figured in the youth and pop culture histories of the past.

The textual practice of the music and youth culture press is indicative of these important changes and displacements. For instance, in Britain in 1987-8 a new magazine based on the independent record sector called *Underground*, took its place amongst the 'style' magazines on the bookstalls. Published by Spotlight publications responsible for *Sounds*, the ailing music magazine weekly rival of *New Musical Express* and *Melody Maker*, *Underground* self-consciously targeted the 'independent young gunslinger' audience and aptly provided the clichéd epitaph for yet another phase in the long demise of the prophesies of the new youth culture. The deliberately amateurish layout, overall design (though carefully crafted) and poor quality paper helped to signify a visible lack of 'style' in direct contrast to *The Face*, *i-D* and *Blitz*. It also contrived to stir popular memory of punk fanzines. A cultural distance was also constructed distinguishing *Underground*'s market from a more upwardly mobile music magazine like *Q* which aimed at an over-25 audience. In line with independent record sales data, 16-25 was the group *Underground* had in mind. From within the media and pop music discourses which have repositioned youth culture since the late 1970s and the early 1980s, *Underground* fashioned a stance against spectacular consumption (in other words against youth culture as 'yuppie' advertising form), comprising a downwardly mobile mood and look. It suggested lack of success, confidence and health rather than the expensive, sporty, vibrant feel of its opponents in the market. Its focus on the local and parochial rather than the metropolitan and cosmopolitan deliberately undercut the smugness of much of Style Culture. It had a keen sense of inherited youth culture discourses, playing on Dick Hebdige's work on subculture and style with a column entitled 'Subculture: the style of meaning.' As its fellow trade papers decline continued in a period where stories of pop permeated the tabloids, *Underground* folded, only to re-emerge for a time as *Offbeat*, a glossier affair still devoted to the same musical movements and audience targets as its predecessor.

By contrast, *Monitor*, was one of the few magazines in the 1980s to ask provocative questions about the possibility of a new pop aesthetic after punk. *Monitor* pointed much more sharply to the the changing rock and pop discourses and youth culture's positioning within them – especially the way in which 'health' became a seam in the rhetoric of pop as much as in politicians' constant references to the 'health' of the economy in general. Looking *unhealthy* and *inefficient* in a culture which has become steeped in hierarchies dependent on valuation of material success, physical fitness, technical proficiency and sexual prowess is in a certain sense to resist, to subvert (however hesitantly) the dominant modes of life and thought in that culture. The histories of rock and pop, and youth culture, since the early 1950s are, increasingly, the raw material for the maintenance and rearticulation of these themes in ideologies which sustain and promote enterprise culture. Their resonance is everywhere in youth styles and pop tastes, though not without their contradictory effects. *Monitor* concentrated on their relationship to musical forms – punk, country, funk, glam, soul – to make sense of them.

The significance of punk is still contested long after its first ripples washed ashore. However, it was, and is, more often than not misread as a street style and folk musical form, as if the music and look represented its subcultural community. Punk music, then, was interpreted as the direct expression of the youthful frustration of the street, the high-rise flats and the dole in mid-1970s Labour Britain. The contrived dissonance of the music was taken as a reflection of the alienation of a subculture, and its principal mode of expression was held to be a gritty 'realism', a faithful reproduction of the noise, disappointment, anger and frustration of urban youth. But as some critics pointed out succintly at the time, 'dole queuers who do identify with punk do so because they share its concern with *play*'[15] not because they believed they could all be spoken for, or represented, by Johnny Rotten or Souxsie. The notion of 'play' has persisted as the key to understanding the connections between rock and pop culture and youth culture, particularly with regard to gender and sexuality in the 1980s, but it is a more and more complex play of 'signs' (musical, historical, political) that is involved in the fundamentally changed conditions in which the various leisure industries now operate. Moreover, this book has questioned the historical basis of subcultural (and to some extent literary) theories of pop, criticising them for their asssumptions of a given, pre-constituted community to be represented in musical form. This is most obvious in the era of Political Pop when disparate groups, subcultures and organisations have been yoked together as a potential 'new bohemia' in the fall-out from a Style Culture which had already been branded as conservative and conformist. However, it is in Post-Political Pop where 'differences' have been recognised, celebrated and defended – where there has been most recognisably a post-'Man' pop culture.

The refusal of citizenship

The playful preference for childlike innocence of some shambling and post-shambling bands has been taken to be signified in a whole range of ways (from the contrived 'girlish' vocals of Talulah Gosh, The Primitives, and The Darling Buds to 1950s anoraks and haircuts) but what matters most is that it involves a desire to keep in mind certain of the 'privileges' of innocence, not an uncontrollable instinct to behave in a puerile fashion. In a culture where, routinely, large sections of youth have been denied access to full time work and, increasingly, fall subject to disciplinary regulation, drawing attention to a state of 'innocence' is politically important. The Thatcher government Social Security legislation which was introduced, and eventually came into force, in the mid-late 1980s penalised young people between 16 and 18 who fail to 'choose' to take up the opportunity of government job training schemes by withdrawing their right to state benefit. The pressure for the imposition of identity cards for young people who wish to drink in pubs (to show they are over 18) , and proposals in the the government scheme (legislated for in the Football Spectators Act) to force the football industry to introduce a compulsory national membership scheme for match attendance in England and Wales fall unjustly and disproportionately on the young. In the current economic and social climate 'youth' has become a significant category for 'disciplining' in social policy. Training policies (Youth Opportunies Programme , Youth Training Scheme, Job Training Scheme and so on) have been widely regarded as 'disciplining' the young unemployed as well as reducing the unemployment statistics for young people. Playing with the notion of 'innocence' – referring to periods of the past forty years when there was seen to be more privilege in being 'young', belonging to 'youth culture', refusing adulthood – amounts to virtually a refusal of citizenship, rather than simply a desire not to grow up. Political status for millions of young people is ever more equivalent to being forced into labour, or more accurately, into a reserve army of labour, especially for the service secrtor as manufacturing industry is run down yet further. An underclass of youth, with severe racial discrimination in jobs built into it, has been created in the developed world which no political ideology proposes to abolish.

In a post-Aids sexual climate, 'innocence' has other sexual and cultural connotations, too. It signifies a looking back to a unspecified period, but one which hinges on the late 1950s and early 1960s axis prior to the 'permissive' age of the later 1960s and 1970s. An interesting example here is Morrissey's cultivation of a legend of androgyny and vague sexual identity which has been underpinned by a thorough-going obsession with the 1960s in music, lyrics and record sleeve design. Morrissey's seemingly endless love affair with 1960s female singers led to his collaboration with Sandie Shaw, who revived her pop career twenty years on by recording Morrissey's songs 'Hand in Glove', 'I Don't Owe You Anything'and 'Jeane' with other members of the band (released by Rough Trade with a cover picture of Rita Tushingham from the 1960s film *A Taste of Honey*). Manchester journalist Mick Middles argued in his much litigated biography of The Smiths that 'Morrissey obviously saw young Sandie as a lead figure to herald a new age of feminism'[16] but the subject himself firmly rejected the claim. Morrissey's similar interest in Oscar Wilde is probably more telling. As with Boy George's much-quoted remarks about his preference for tea drinking over sexual encounters, the delight in playing games of truth with a touchingly naive, and yet ruthlessly exploitative, press overrode any desire to reveal essential sexual or political identities. It is noteworthy, though, that 'Morrissey didn't take it to the limit. He wasn't stupid. He knew that he was marketing a lifestyle; he knew that if he actually said "I would prefer to go to bed with a man than a woman" then he would have gone too far'.[17] Bands such as The Man From Delmonte have been caught by just such moral censure for their more explicit gay lyrics. Morrissey's ascetism, however mannered, is nevertheless, of some importance. It parallels the Greek conception of self which Michel Foucault portrayed in his history of sexuality where he studied the practices by which individuals in antiquity were led to focus the attention on themselves to decipher, recognise and acknowledge themselves as subjects of desire, or lack of desire. What Foucault concentrated on – at least in the later volumes of this project – was the history of what he called 'techniques of self' emphasising that part of the human condition in antiquity, modernity and postmodernity has been a making of 'subjects' of various different kinds. Aids has forced just such an invention of new subjectivities on to the agenda. Youth culture, and notions of the new bohemia, are manifestly part of the proliferating discourses on pop, sexuality and consumption that form the 'technologies of the self' and 'micro-powers' which in turn discipline and govern the populations of the West. They are explicitly discourses of excess, of overexposure, of hyper-consumption. Against these 'regimes of truth' there is also the possibility of new practices of the self. The scope for invention and adoption of these new subjectivities, rather than the attempt to 'represent' divided or non-existent communities, is what makes Post-Political Pop significant today.

Both in the fields of sexuality and the politics of youth we have seen the crisis of meanings associated with youth subculture analysis, in particular regarding its relationship to popular music. What is evident is a profound questioning of the notion of the 'liberation of youth'. But it is clear that this meta-narrative has sustained subcultural theories of pop since the 1950s. One of the most prominent Centre for Contemporary Cultural Studies authors in the 1970s, Paul Willis, has more recently continued to argue for this 'emancipation of youth', especially in relation to political parties who claim to represent youth:

> My plea to Labour is simple. Let us commit ourselves to the emancipation of youth. Let us stop thinking of youth issues only as an after-thought to what adults think are the main issues. Let us stop collecting a rag bag of bits from other policy areas and putting a belated youth gloss on it. Let us put youth in the vanguard of a new kind of socialism, a new kind of state.[18]

It is precisely such a 'meta-narrative' – that of the 'liberation of youth'- which is one of the most dominant of post-war mythologies in the West. It is a claim which is in increasing danger of critique and ridicule as we approach the end of the century and such theoretical explanations – and their objects – become more and more fragmented. The 'liberation' of youth, as with, for example, the liberation of 'sexuality', assumes a unified subject of such discourses which can be (re)constituted by policies designed to reveal its truth. It is especially fraught with difficulty in its attempt to explicate the relations between deviant youth subcultures and popular music. A whole series of specific discourses – economic, geographical, political, musical –

interpellate the 'subject' of youth culture with radically conflicting cultural messages. It needs to be remembered, too, that any narrative of *the end* of the 'emancipation of youth' story is still a meta-narrative and is caught out by the critics who point to the incompatability between such all embracing explanations or stories and the condition of postmodernity.

However, as has been claimed throughout this book, it is not necessary to rely on the 'counter-discourses' first generated around pop and rock music culture in the late 1960s in order to make sense of pop and rock culture and youth culture. 'Counter-cultures' is now more resonant of shopping and consumption rather than resistance and deviance. In particular, the earlier analysis of the media formation of Political Pop should remind us that the issues of 'representation' and 'folk ideology' in pop and rock discourse are no longer clear cut, and that, as has been seen in this Chapter, no new rebellious, deviant, self-generating, youth culture or youth subculture can be said to pre-exist the formation of Political Pop, and therefore to be represented by it. Nevertheless, as Jacques Attali has shown,[19] music can pre-figure social formations in an important way: a 'new bohemia' does not have to constitute itself as a new youth (sub)culture in order for it to have a significant social and political function; it does not need to be represented by specific musical instutions and forms. As Fredric Jameson argues in his foreword to Attali's book, 'whatever our judgement on the details of his own analysis', Attali's 'conception of music as prophetic of the emergent social, political, and economic forms of a radically different society can thus be an energising one.' In the next Chapter, we need to consider, in the context of one moment of pop history, this enticing possibility.

5

Don't go back rockville: post-political pop

Theorists of postmodern culture and postmodernism have justifiably focused on the crisis in cultural and political authority of the West. Pop and rock music culture, and the attendant sexual and political discourses which have underpinned it, have developed in a post-war world which has witnessed increasing global concentration of the production and distribution of the commodities associated with popular music, and an ever more integral relationship between the various leisure and cultural industries. Rock and pop's cultural power, for instance, the perceived capacity to bind people in community, has been achieved through an Anglo-American musical form which, from the beginning, has plagiarised and re-worked diverse traditional, roots and folk musics. Its longevity has been sustained by a proliferation of discourses and practices which have created, then taken as their object, a social space in a particular phase of Pop Time occupied by youth culture. Since the 1970s there have frequently been proclamations of the 'end of youth culture' and the 'death of rock culture', forcing a re-evaluation of past orthodoxies on 'rebellious' or 'deviant' youth, and rock and pop's potential.

Rapping the postmodern

This book has taken issue with certain theorisations of postmodernism and popular music, which have tended either to concentrate on the *correspondence* between the 'postmodern condition' and 'late capitalism' or else celebrate the spectacular consumption represented by modern youth styles. Drawing on contemporary material the book has analysed certain trends in popular music and youth culture since the demise of New Pop and suggested an alternative mapping of the cultural politics of pop, youth culture and deviance.

The tendency which links late capitalism to postmodernism is most clearly represented in the work of Fredric Jameson, who has regarded what he sees as the dominant 'cultural logic' of late capitalism with a rather ambivalent hostility. This tendency assumes a cultural pessimism, whilst maintaining a version of Marxism as historical materialist method. The most directly relevant references in this body of work are, amongst other artists such as Talking Heads and Laurie Anderson, to The Clash as 'postmodern pop'. Such theorisation of postmodernism and pop takes no account of the most important developments since punk, especially those associated with rap and hip-hop, house and reggae. Contrary to this first tendency there is a line of thought which concentrates on 'post-subcultural' styles and replaces Jameson's pessimism with a cultural optimism. Whereas Jameson's focus is more on a politics of production, there is in cultural optimism a stress on the politics of consumption, and, moreover, a marked – though critical – celebration of spectacular consumption. The foremost representatives of such work are Dick Hebdige and Iain Chambers[1]. As in the personal academic biographies of Hebdige and Chambers, their later work represents a move away from the initial theoretical positions developed in studies of youth subcultures in the Centre for Contemporary Cultural Studies in the mid-1970s. Whereas Jameson stresses Marxist methodology, Hebdige and Chambers draw, as well as on Marxist-influenced cultural theorists such as Walter Benjamin, on French postmodern theory as developed by Jean Baudrillard and Paul Virilio.

Along with, for instance, Jean-François Lyotard's quite different writings on (post)modernism, it is Jean Baudrillard's work which has become the latest in a long line of Continental imports into Anglo-American cultural theory. This is, of course, precisely the reverse of the process by which Anglo/American popular culture (in the form of rock and pop) has colonised the world, though the intermingling and cross-cultural transmission of cultural and intellectual commodities is much more complex. Paris has become the centre of the transmission of world music and some parts of Euro-pop have taken over from American rock as the leading, cutting edge of the popular cultural form. The present fashion for the Left Bank, as with previous fads, has its pitfalls. Baudrillard, in particular, evades his would-be followers in a series of ever more perplexing moves as former partisans in various academic cultures have discovered. It has indeed been argued, justifiably, that one cannot be a 'Baudrillardian in the way that one can be a Marxian.'[2] Moreover, despite certain powerful and challenging insights which Baudrillard makes with regard to the changing contemporary contours of the 'social', there is little likelihood of moving directly from his deeply introspective ventures to an incisive analysis of the restructuring and realignment of new cultural and political forces. Dick Hebdige has pointed to the problematic attraction of Baudrillard's work as a whole:

> I must say that I feel very ambivalent about Baudrillard, because in one sense I realise the pertinence of what he is saying. But I also have my suspicions that the kind of will motivating his work seems to be poisonous. I'm not setting him up as the enemy, because in many ways he sets up his own disappearance. To talk about it in ecological terms, the language he uses is not very fruitful, there's not much future in it.[3]

Baudrillard certainly plays a contradictory role in the two schools of Cultural Studies which we have identified as 'cultural pessimism' and 'cultural optimism'. Whilst Jameson acknowledges the significance of Baudrillard, the general tenor of postmodernism is seen as negative in cultural pessimism. Cultural optimists, however, have sought to use Baudrillard more positively. In terms of pop's social and sonic history, though, there is a line of convergence between Baudrillard's observation about history not being 'over', but rather appearing 'in a state of simulation', and the current pop tendency to visit and revisit the thousands of sounds from the musical cultures of the global village. It is also to be found in the desire in youth culture to quote and rework the past of subcultural politics and history through the ubiquitous androgynous signs of leather jackets, Doc Martens, Levi 501 jeans (ripped or not) and short back and sides (flat-top or not) haircuts.

At the time of Jameson's claims on behalf of The Clash, in the mid-1980s, pop music history had shifted dramatically. To what extent this has helped us to 'map the postmodern', however, is a more complicated question than Jameson's confusing citation of The Clash might suggest. For Jameson, in the 1980s, pastiche was everywhere; a condition in which there is a pervasive attempt to recall a time less problematic than our own, and a consequent refusal to engage the present or think historically, producing, what he calls, a schizophrenia of consumer society. Hal Foster, in his book on postmodern culture which included contributions from Baudrillard and Jameson amongst others, argues that cultural politics today comprises one postmodernism which 'deconstructs' modernism and the status quo (in other words a postmodernism of 'resistance') and another postmodernism which is a reaction against modernism even constituting a strategic rejection of modernism pointing to it as the cause of the problems of modernisation (in other words a postmodernism of 'neo-conservatism'). A postmodern resistance is here set up by Foster as a critical deconstruction of tradition, not a pastiche of historical forms; it is not a return to origins but a critique of both what he sees as the official culture of modernism and the false promises of reactionary postmodernism. By the end of the 1980s such a triangle seemed less and less tenable, especially in the context of popular music. Part of the problem with Jameson's analysis is his critical rejection of pastiche. Pastiche is ever-present in pop history. Moreover it could be argued that it helps to recreate cultural experiences as well as awakening a sense of the past. The use of past styles in popular music is not simply escapism; it is not just a reactionary nostalgia of the kind which Jameson focuses on in his criticism of some forms of postmodernism. Furthermore, quotation, parody, allusion, self-referentiality – all figures which are cited as signalling the dominance of postmodern – are also integral to popular music history; they do not simply suddenly appear in the post-punk era. Jameson's romanticism leads him to see in punk an uncommodified 'British working class rock' which predates, in his terms, a further slide into postmodernism. In fact, neither 1970s punk nor 1980s folk/country/roots can be seen as either simply a resistance to commodification, or else as a form of reactionary escapism.

The problem for theorists of the postmodern condition, who wish to draw on postmodern theory to analyse their object particularly in regard to popular music, is the glut of signs, the very excess of rock and pop discourse which prevails. The postmodern 'subject' is bombarded by all sorts of signs. That does, however, mean that there can still be a concentration on one particular discourse, relying on it as a privileged way of representing experience – an obsession with 1960s pop 'innocence' is one example, as was seen in Chapter 4. The mass of conflicting cultural messages which subjects have to select, arrange and re-arrange is precisely what Baudrillard is theorising in his notion of the 'ecstasy of communication'. The problem is to know what this selection process consists of: in a sense, how do audiences read the myriad pop signs? How do they shift their readings in different contexts and different historical periods? In what way are they bricoleurs? Baudrillard argues that the relationship of the 'masses' to the media has changed so that the masses fail to respond, other than passively, to the media messages. This 'radical' subversion of the 'social' for Baudrillard is a cause of celebration, since it is a way of seeing the masses playing, jokily, with the media. But, as Dick Hebdige rightly points out, it is politically debilitating to engage in this kind of dangerous brinkmanship since this theorisation supposedly encompasses the 'end' of subjectivity, prompting the widespread notion that postmodernism inevitably involves the transformation of the subject into a mere 'screen'. This book has assumed, against Baudrillard's argument, that the 'social' has not disappeared; in the sense that Baudrillard means it, the media has not displaced it. But it has been taken for granted in the analysis of the media formation of Political Pop and the connected 'disappearance' of the new bohemia that major changes are indeed taking place in the cultural industries which continue to display some of the characteristics that Baudrillard attributes to postmodernity – for example, hyperreality. A theory of the politics of pop which does not entail the destructive potential of Baudrillard's theorisation of the media needs to take seriously the 'refusal of citizenship' which was considered in Chapter 4 without elevating it to the status of a 'fatal strategy' as Baudrillard would do. It is therefore a political problem to be overcome rather than a cause for celebration.

Textural practice

Part of the difficulty with the analysis of musical discourses and texts is that rock and pop criticism has not exactly constituted itself as a major critical practice to be taken seriously in the way that drama and film theory have been. One reason for this is rock culture's relative youthfulness: 'rockville' – rock theory, rock culture, a 'rock' sound – is a post-war phenomenon. Forty years is a short time in which to build a 'canon of rock musical criticism'.[4] Moreover, such cultural and political evaluation that it has managed to achieve has varied considerably: over time – the 1970's were in many ways more productive than the 1960s; and with place – compared with Britain, the United States of America has tended to accord a more academic 'space' to rock and pop writing. Essentially, though, it remains the lowest of 'low culture' theory in contrast to criticism of literature, painting, theatre, classical music and opera. To take it, and its object, seriously (as with many other forms of popular culture) is to risk becoming the subject of ridicule from *both* those who want to relax in front of the soap opera, football match or 'pop' television show whilst switching off their critical faculties, and the fans whose almost universal response is to ask why should anyone take seriously an activity which is perceived to be for 'fun'. However, there are indications since the late 1970s that popular music and, more importantly its theories and its histories, are likely to receive more sustained analytical attention.

Even in a 'high theory' book in a well regarded 'high theory' series, Alan Durant[5] saw fit to devote a lengthy chapter to 'Rock Today', although it did concentrate overmuch on a particular period in the 1970s, rather than the 1980s when it was written and published, and ended up formulating a programme of future work rather than a finished canon. An international umbrella organisation (IASPM – the International Association For The Study of Popular Music) has been in existence since the early 1980s, and several new centres have been created, or extended, within the academy – for instance in Britain at the Universities of Liverpool, and Glasgow and Strathclyde – to further the focus on pop and theory. The most prominent theorist/critics have opened up a political field for such cultural analysis in a wide range of publications from art journals such as *Art and Text* and *Artforum* to mass circulation newspapers such the as the *Observer* and the *Independent* and periodicals like the *New Statesman and Society* and *Village Voice*. Meanwhile, the conventional music press struggles to overcome this very tension: how to write about ephemeral trends – and indeed to keep on manufacturing them – without leaving readers either stupefied at the language that is used, or just plain bored. The partial shift of *Melody Maker* in the mid-1980s from macho weekly to a more wordy, serious paper was largely due to the recruitment of young writers from the Oxford-University-based fanzine *Monitor* which we discussed in Chapter 4 as representing a monument to experimental writing on pop theory in the earlier part of the decade. The readers' letters column in *Melody Maker* in the period from 1985 to 1987 is a testament to the mixture of bewilderment, anger and excitement that such an editorial move invoked.

That such renewed energy in the field of cultural and political analysis of pop music culture has led to difficulties – of comprehension, of argument and even employment – is clear. What is more awkward to establish is the relationship between the kinds of explanations, terms and concepts which have been used in, say the literary field or film studies, and a cultural form which is acknowledged by the writers themselves to be valuable precisely because of its frequently trivial or fleeting nature. Literary studies on the one hand, subcultural theory on the other, have acted as the mainstays of theories of popular music since the 1960s: both, however, underwent substantial re-examination in the 1980s. Our analysis of Political Pop as a social formation was based on just such critique. Increasingly the argument that such theory is inappropriate to pop practice – and that new theory consequently needs to be developed – is making itself heard.[6]

This book has sought to develop some of these themes in a specific account of a recent conjuncture in pop music culture and its legal and social regulation: when what had become known, ambiguously, as the New Pop finally lost its grip on pop consciousness, and indeed conscience. The best theoretical analyses of pop and rock and youth culture were written and published before the unfolding of this particular snatch of Pop Time. What has come, instead, to dominate rock and pop discourse in these years is a populist reaction *against* theory. On the one hand, there is a 'left' populism (for instance, represented by writers such as Robin Denselow and Adam Sweeting in the *Guardian*) which apparently eschews theory in favour of a descriptive, factual account of new releases, concerts and artists, but which is implicitly governed by the writers' notion of how and why pop matters. The emphasis differs depending on which historical period of pop is seen as most significant, dictating which artists might be singled out for special treatment – for instance, in the case of these particular writers, respectively, Richard Thompson, or Simple Minds. But the general view is that rock and pop *are* important, and can be mobilised for good causes. On the other hand there, is a 'right' populism which denies the significance of pop and rock, and mocks any serious attention given to them. The tabloid press pop pages, the majority of BBC Radio 1 disc jockeys and many other pundits share such a perspective. Julie Burchill – predictably – expressed it, in a review of Simon Frith and Howard Horne's venture into 'art theory' and 'pop practice' when she claimed that:

> The recent interests of academics in pop has had very little effect on the way ordinary young people think about and use pop music outside the seminar room. There are two reasons. One is that serious intellectual discussion about pop music smacks patronisingly of the trendy vicar or swinging teacher – 'The Pistols, man'. The second is that advanced young moderns do not, thank goodness, really *think* about pop music anymore. It has moved to the periphery, where it belongs; background music to make love and money to.[7]

What such an account conveniently glosses over (beyond the rightward shift of the author's own musings) is the specific economic, political and cultural changes over the last decade which have made it possible for this 'right' populism to become popular. At the very moment when pop and rock are so pervasive in our contemporary culture, to assert that its marginality makes rigorous analysis improper is perverse.

What divides these populist angles most obviously is the division 'rock' and 'pop'. These are important 'low culture' terms which have come to underline the serious/periphery divide: a kind of high/low division *within* popular music criticism. There is obscured, though, an ideological and economic struggle over these theoretical terms in the history of the pop process itself. Also, both populisms have in common an avowed resistance to theoretical analysis. This book has taken their own analyses seriously as part of the 'texts' which make up rock and pop discourse, and attempted to develop a theoretical argument which sets their own instrumental standpoints ('rock' as a useful tool, 'pop' as a background object) in the overall cultural politics of pop today. We have, however, argued here that 'textual' analysis alone cannot produce an effective appraisal of the rock, pop and folk ideologies at work in this pop moment. Pop musical 'texts' are too often laughably misunderstood.[8] Words are discretely 'read' as if they were the equivalent of poetry, when what really counts is their place in textures of sound. Such sound textures, too, are not independent of the production, distribution and consumption of the various commodities associated with the music and diverse other culture and leisure industries, or of the exploitation of the property rights associated with these commodities. Equally, though, a more straightforward sociological account of the context, or conditions of production, of musical forms is insufficient and frequently misleading.

The fact is that pop music culture is an 'impossible' object; if it ever could, it can certainly no longer be taken as 'given' that we know what it looks like. Rather it needs to be mapped, as in these Chapters, by revealing the discourses and practices that constitute it. It is only then, by seeing something of its ever-changing shape, that its policing and regulation can be understood.

The Chapters in this book have attempted to theorise and explain the formation of Political Pop in the period from around 1983 onwards, and, more importantly, the combination of diverse elements which make up the barely visible traces of its opposite, Post-Political Pop. Far from being simply seen as either a barren period of 'pop'n'politics', or alternatively an optimistic renewal of pop's social role, these formations form a complex point in cultural politics. As Pop Time becomes ever shorter and in scarce supply, the market demands of the music and media industries for global expansion create a series of tensions in the cultural meaning of pop and rock.

However, the central issue is, as Dave Haslam says,whether it can still – or ever – be said that popular 'music can achieve something'. More-over, the much vaunted return to a new authenticity is predicated on the idea of 'rock values', a presumption of a pre-existing 'rock culture'. As Haslam argues, on the question of:

music achieving something, if that achievement is measured in terms which are basically rock values, then you're missing out on whole areas of experience of music, music which I feel very strongly about, which you know is good music, but not measured by rock values. But there's no sense that I want the streets to be filled with banner waving fans of those types of music in order to feel that those types of music have succeeded. One of the things I've learnt from DJ-ing – take a record like The Turntable Orchestra 'You're gonna miss me when I go' which is a great record. If you try to measure that in terms of rock values, then you're going to end up off the mark. When you put that record on and it fills the dance floor you know that those people who have been queueing for half an hour to get into the club, who have paid £3 to get in there, are having the best time of the week – that record can be the highlight of the week – and that's its achievement, and my achievement as a DJ. Its obviously the role of the DJ to find those records, and to work those records, and to make records like that happen often enough, as many times as possible, as many nights of the week as possible. In that kind of world the identity of who the Turntable Orchestra are – whether they're black or white, where do they live? who are they? do they do gigs? are they on Rough Trade records? what is the political opinion of the people behind the record? does the singer write the music? or does he just sing? is he writing from experience? – none of that you know. And none of that you need to know, in order for that record to work. Whereas rock values would suggest that in order to like that record you have to like what the singer says about a political subject, or you have to know that the favourite records of The Turntable Orchestra are also your favourite records, so you can feel like you're part of a movement.

This need for a particular kind of mediation in rock culture is, for Haslam, the:

basic difference between The Turntable Orchestra 'You're gonna miss me when I go' and say The Smiths 'Bigmouth Strikes Again'; they're on the same label, they're on Rough Trade. And they're probably promoted by the same publicity people. There are lots of connections. But at the point where they meet the music fan, there is almost no way the parallel could meet. There's no connection betwewen the experience. The Smiths' fans demanded something different than the music they like, compared with someone who comes to a dance club. To me they're neither of them 'mainstream' records – both of them reached the lower reaches of the charts, both of them are classics, both of them work, both are examples of good music.[9]

The 'contexts' of rock and pop 'texts', then, are indeed crucial in understanding what pleasures are produced for consumers, what desires are satisfied. Consumers who listen to their purchases at home after, or during, reading about them in the media are part of a cultural experience different from consumers who listen to music while they are dancing in a club – even if it is the same record. For a cultural theorist like Lawrence Grossberg, however, all such texts are constituted by what he calls the discourse of the rock and roll apparatus. The effects of these texts depend on the fact that such apparatus functions at different levels of social life and power. 'Rock' produces, for Grossberg, sites of 'affective empowerment' which can provide strategies of resistance, evasion and even counter-control. The argument in this book is that even if this were the case, what needs to be known is the history of the way these specific discourses of rock and pop are constituted, and the manner in which they compete in the construction of cultural meaning in any particular period of pop history. What also becomes relevant, here, is the division between those who argue for what might be called 'cultural practice' and those who focus on 'signifying practice'. An analysis such as Alan Durant's falls into the former category because it would see the material conditions of the performance and of the audience as crucial for understanding the meaning of rock and pop texts – in other words, it is necessary to explain the background context of the music industry, the club, concert hall and so on to grasp the meaning of any musical performance. 'Signifying practice', in contrast, would demand the analysis of music in terms of it being 'structured like a language', as the pyschoanalytic theorist Jacques Lacan argued. For 'signifying practice' to be the dominant focus in music criticism the production of 'subject positions' from where texts can be 'read' needs to be analysed. In this argument, a regime of representation constructs the place(s) of reading, the points of viewing. The problem with both of these approaches to popular music is that it is sound *textures* rather than simply texts, which are being talked or written about. Combining the focus on both 'signifying' and 'cultural' practice still leaves this issue unresolved. The precise nature of the musical space that has provided historically determined postions for the subject of rock and pop discourse is always elusive.

Produced and abandoned

One such example of this musical space, which in Jacques Attali's sense prefigures rather than reflects a politics of pop, is the work of Adrian Sherwood. Though elements of what we have called Post-Political Pop appear and reappear in all kinds of music inside the formation Political Pop, Sherwood's productions are an excellent example of its contours. Adrian Sherwood, producer and On-Sound record label owner, has used rock, dub reggae, funk and hip-hop rhythms to create a place for poular music sounds which go way beyond the subversion of William Burroughs' tape cut-ups or even the much hailed avant-garde of New York 'No Wave' rock artists such as Lydia Lunch and Glenn Branca, whose influence is detectable in bands like Sonic Youth.[10] As Dele Fadele says in the 20 page booklet that accompanied a various artistes album featuring On-U Sound musicians and singers, *Pay it all Back*, Vol 2, released in 1988:

> Trading in speed and velocity these motley crews (like Singers and Players, Gary Clail, Barmy Army, Tackhead, Keith Le Blanc, Lee 'Scratch' Perry) imitate the seizures of madness like the trajectory of some rocket's flight-path. It's all down to the edit. In this summer of Acid House, their skull duggery and clandestine tactics make them peerless. Sampling is fast becoming an overused term, almost a gimmick, but you can hear On-U Sound's influences on the field at large and some spreading global network that links Chicago, Berlin, London and New York in some nomadic quest for light and shadow.

The immediate pop context of Sherwood's work is important. As against Fredric Jameson's citation of punk band The Clash (alongside the much more relevant post-punk group The Gang of Four) as one instance of 'postmodern pop', it was Big Audio Dynamite – the band formed by ex-Clash guitarist Mick Jones – who provided a more contemporary example at the time of Jameson's theoretical intervention. Despite the decline of the band's recordings, their early output displayed a subtle mix of African, hip-hop, reggae, and white rock styles, together with junk noise from the post-industrial urban soundscape, predating the obsession with such pop tourism which came to pervade club and chart styles in the late 1980s. Albums such as *This Is ... BAD* , released on CBS in 1985, provided a premature social and political documentary – the sound, rather than the substance, of the new bohemia – in which, amongst others, Roxanne Shante, Salt'n'Pepa, Cookie Crew and Wee Papa Girl Rappers supplied a counter to the overt macho style (including ubiquitous crotch-grabbing) personified by the likes of LL Cool J, the now deceased Scott La Rock, NWA (Niggers With Attitude) and the much more overtly 'political' (in a black muslim sense) Public Enemy. On a different plane, Run DMC, Cold Cut, Scratchmo and Eric B and Rakim, for instance, relied on stolen sounds from, respectively, heavy metal (Aerosmith), classic soul (James Brown), some vintage jazz (Louis Armstrong) and Israeli female vocal (Ofra Haza). Further, the chart success of disc jockey based outfits like S-Express and Bomb The Bass, and singers like Yazz and Neneh Cherry, showed how the underground dance scene can often, initially, be more important than national radio airplay.

Adrian Sherwood's own career began as a teenage disc jockey in the 1970s, and On-U Sound was eventually established in 1980. Remarkable for its sheer survival and constant mutation of its high quality crew of singers and players, On-U Sound is a landmark of what might be described as Post-Political Pop. This is, partly, a matter of production and distribution of commodities; a stern, resolute, opposition to being dominated and controlled by large multinational conglomerates. Sherwood argues[11] that despite the loss of money (with many others) when Northern distributors for the Cartel, Red Rhino, went into bankruptcy, and increasing despair at the state of the music industry, there should still be a commitment to producing sounds at 'the edges' of popular music. Resisting the temptations to become swallowed up by the industry as an employed producer, he has continued to work with what he regards as the best purveyors of rhythms – former Sugarhill Gang 'house' band, Keith Le Blanc, Doug Wimbish and Skip McDonald – who have formed the basis of Tackhead, Barmy Army, and the Maffia; or Roots Radics drummer Style Scott; or legendary dub master Lee 'Scratch' Perry. Mixing funk, dub, reggae, hip-hop and other styles with hundreds of 'found sounds', Sherwood's production sound is elusive and compelling. As Dele Fadele says in his sleeve notes homage:

> As empires crumble and the patriarchy weakens, dub-language files back reports in communiques in which understanding isn't the main priority ...

Dub is amnesia made concrete to the clatter of six-gun ricochets. And Adrian Sherwood has taken this methodology into new realms with electronic washes and the certainty of knowing what's left out of the sonic-picture is most important. What remains can be assessed in many ways, none of them reliable – that's the paradox. Earthquakes, stabilized economies, treasury crimes, the shroud of communism, displacement, colonization, scrubland, ice deserts, wide-open spaces, depth charges all come to mind when describing the visceral impact of his output. And there's politics to spare, couched in the language of cut-ups, fold-ins, drop-outs. William Burroughs' much-vaunted tape experiments have nothing on Tackhead's missile emotion dance floor stormers, they just form the basic inspiration blocks. As contemporary music disappears up its own arse by re-entering the dark ages, we welcome you to the precipice. One more step and everything goes up in smoke, both ends burning.

Nowhere is this enterprise shown better than on Sherwood's 'soccer' songs – Barmy Army tracks, and Tackhead's single 'The Game'. There are, occasionally, worthy popular music examples of celebration of the pleasures of football (the Real Sounds of Africa 'Tornados vs Dynamos 3-3', for instance), or football fans' indignation at government interference – for instance, the compilation album against the Football Spectators Act, *Bananas*, in association with the football fanzine *Rodney Rodney*. Sherwood's ubiquitous use of soccer chant samples is, however, quite different. On the On-U Sound single eventually released in 1988, 'Sharp As A Needle/England 2 Yugoslavia 0', there was created a disembodied 'community singing' for a disembodied community. Instead of trying to represent a locality, region or subculture, Sherwood's mix of 'Abide With Me', sampled TV noise and terrace chants (such as the post-Falklands version of Ee-Ay-Addio 'We've Won the War') captured a blend of passion, pride, regionalism and nationalism by deconstructing, and then reconstituting, the various, diverse elements. Not representation so much as presenting the unpresentable.

At the end of the century, and indeed at the end of the millenium, such 'music to end the world to' is increasingly the only music which makes much political sense. Music which is 'political' in the sense of lyrical correctness, or reflection of the stance of a social or political grouping, is, as can be seen from the experience of Political Pop, inevitably dependent on the larger social formations of the time for its effects. Alternatively, attempts at a re-introduction of politics 'back' into pop risk essentialising contemporary popular music (say 'folk', 'world' or 'roots') as fundamentally separable from the commercial pop process as represented by 'mainstream' chart music, and therefore somehow 'post', or outside, pop. Post-Political Pop, on the other hand, by deconstructing pop history, and rearticulating its constituents in new, formative ways is able to contribute to what the cultural theorist Raymond Williams called 'a new kind of assessment of the basic meanings of human history'. Williams suggested in his book *Towards 2000* that:

> The assessment is complex and self-conscious but also often anxious. Some people find reassurance in this long past, in which so much has been achieved, in so many different forms, and so many dangers and limitations have been surmounted. Others, in effect, escape into it, spinning time backwards from what they see as a hopeless present and a short and disastrous future.[12]

The absolute non-end

This book has tried to find some answers to the problem of what happened to the relationship between popular music, youth culture and deviance in the years since punk. In the 1950s, 1960s and 1970s pop and rock music seemed inextricably connected to a never-ending succession of deviant youth subcultures – teds, rockers, mods, hippies, skinheads, rastas, punks. However in the Thatcher Years of the 1980s youth culture became more of an advertising medium than ever before; it was notable not for opposition, but for its role in selling everything from Levi 501 jeans to spot cream. Proclamations were frequently made in the 1980s about the end of youth culture, the death of rock culture and the new conservative (and Conservative) conformism of youth. Adulthood was in; so, too, were flaunting material success, postmodernism and the enterprise culture. Radicalism, rebellion and resistance were confined to the dustbin of history. They were replaced by Style Culture, looking good and feeling healthy. The music became safe along with the culture – background sounds to make love or money to. From the beat generation (according to Matt Johnson of The The) to the beaten generation. Or so we were told.

This book has offered an alternative perspective on popular music and youth culture in the 1980s and beyond. Although it has presented the material in a variety of different ways, reflecting a suitable postmodern mixture of pop seriousness and academic trivia, it is in fact based on interviews with disc jockeys, record label owners, musicians, producers, writers and fans. It has described and analysed the shift in cultural dominance from New Pop in the early 1980s to what it called Political Pop in the mid-late 1980s. This movement involved a change in pop thinking and rock theory, a move from an obsession with style, looks, packaging and synthetic sounds to content, socially conscious lyrics, honesty and a new rock-oriented authenticity – in short to a pop humanism, to a caring rock music. However spurious and uneven this move, pop and rock definitions, and their use, changed dramatically as the rightward surge in political, economic and social fields gathered pace. Crucially, the new pop media formation of Political Pop in turn produced its own deviant offspring, Post-Political Pop. Post-Political Pop can be spotted in some of the cut-ups, drop-ins and dance floor terrorism of Adrian Sherwood's On-U Sound productions; or the country/punk and surrealism of long-time survivors The Mekons; or the 'Northern folk' of The Fall and King of The Slums; or the all-round pop 'entertainment' of Elvis Costello. But it is much more pervasive than such snapshots might suggest. More than this, Post-Political Pop continues the lost link between popular music and deviance. It points the way for a re-introduction of politics into pop as we rapidly approach the end of the century, and indeed the millennium. Importantly, it does not succumb to a fruitless search for a new punk or a new politics of youth, despite the appearance of fresh figures of youth culture and deviance – for instance, casuals, B-Boys, Acid Housers and lager louts.

Finally, this book began with reference to a poster from Manchester's most famous recent popular or youth cultural landmark, the Haçienda. However, it is not this venue, nor even the G-Mex Centre – where in 1986 the city's nostalgia buffs celebrated the tenth summer since punk – or, for that matter any of the other plentiful sites of pleasure, pop and politics in any particular (sub)urban space and time that we should longingly remember. The sign that always caught the eye when I was researching and writing this book was at none of these more obvious places, but above a second-hand 'junk' (mainly musical) shop on Oxford Road run by Johnny Roadhouse. The legend above the shop has read for many years: 'I Buy Anything' and 'I Buy I Buy I Buy I Buy I Buy I Buy'. This Baudrillardian excess, this intimation of hyper-consumption – albeit downbeat – seemed to fit the epitaph for the book better than any other. Consumption crises come and go, in rapid circulation, but the fast separating spheres of pop and youth culture are inextricably bound to this nexus.

The simplest answer to the question 'whatever happened to punk?' which pervades this book – in other words, what became of pop's seemingly perennial connection to deviance – is that a whole series of new authenticities[1] have indeed been produced, each corresponding more or less to market segments, each subject to increasingly speedy change and transformation. Moreover, the new fault lines of rock and pop discourse are not so much 'rock/pop', 'authentic/synthetic', 'true/false' – privileging high culture over low culture in terms of musical or artistic value as Adorno and the Frankfurt school would have it – but rather 'global/local'. It is the deconstruction, of this couplet in the process of its own production and consumption which makes Post-Political Pop worth taking seriously.

Notes, references and select discography

The select discography for each Chapter is not meant to be comprehensive of artists or musical styles. It merely serves as a supplementary playlist, or soundtrack - an indication of what the book should sound like. The best way to read it is with the accompaniment of two albums produced by Adrian Sherwood: one which takes its name from this book, Gary Clail On-U Sound Sound System *End of the Century Party*; and the other the best 'football' record ever made, Barmy Army: *The English Disease.*

A 'post'-script

1 'Drinking and Disorder : A Study of Non-Metropolitan Violence', *Home office research study* 108, 1989.
2 See A. Kroker and M. Kroker: *Body invaders: sexuality and the postmodern condition* (Macmillan, London, 1988), A. Kroker and D. Cook: *The postmodern scene: excremental culture and hyper-aesthetics* (Macmillan, London, 1988) and A. Kroker, M. Kroker and D. Cook: *Panic encyclopaedia* (Macmillan, London, 1989). See also S. Lotringer: *Overexposed* (Pantheon, New York, 1988).

For a tongue-in-chic antidote to the media excess, play My Life With The Thrill Kill Cult : 'Nervous Xians/The Devil Does Drugs' (Wax Trax); for News at Ten theme and more, Renegade Sound Wave: 'The Kray Twins' (Rhythm King); Front 242: *Official Version* (RRE) is a good example of the sound of what has been dubbed 'New Beat' - in existence since the early 1980s despite the media label being applied only in the late 1980s; for a good sampler including Front 242 and Canadian outfit Skinny Puppy, see Various Artists: *This is Electronic Body Music* (Ediesta); a useful introduction to various styles of contemporary dance (hip-hop, house, garage) is found on Various Artists: *Upfront 9* (Serious), and Soul II Soul: *Club Classics Vol 1* (10); see also A Guy Called Gerald: 'Voodoo Ray' (Rham) and *Hot Lemonade* (Rham), and 808 State: *Newbuild* and *Quadrastate* (Creed); for the (post)modern sound of Detroit, see Various Artists: *Techno*(10); and for the North of England, see Various Artists: *Freak Beats Vol 1: a tacky souvenir of pre-revolutionary Northern England* (Scam/Bop Cassettes).

Chapter 1

1 J. Baudrillard: 'Hunting Nazis' in *New statesman*, February 19, 1988
2 See T. Young: 'The Fall of the House of Style' in *New society*, August 2, 1985, and 'The Fashion Victims' in *New society*, March 14, 1986.
3 T. Young: 'The Shock of the Old' in *New society*, February 14, 1985, p.246.
4 A. Martin and G. Hayes : 'The Eighties (A Fragment)' in E.Grosz et al (eds): *Futur*fall: excursions into post-modernity* (Power Institute of Fine Art, Sydney, 1986), p.164.
5 Ibid., p.161.
6 S. Frith: *Sound effects* (Constable, London, 1983), p.51.
7 Ibid., p.52.
8 C. MacCabe: 'Broken English' in C.MacCabe (ed): *Futures for English* (Manchester University Press, Manchester, 1988), p.9.
9 A. Goodwin: 'Music Video in the (Post)Modern World' in *Screen* Vol 28 No 3, 1987, especially pp.48-52.
10 See for different emphasis within this dichotomy, S. Rijven et al: *Rock for ethiopia* (IASPM Working Paper 7, 1985), D. Hebdige: *Hiding in the light: on images and things* (Routledge/Comedia, London, 1988), Ch.9, and S. Hall: *The hard road to renewal* (Verso, London, 1988), Ch.17.
11 See, for a critical summary, M. Cousins and A. Hussain: *Michel Foucault* (Macmillan, London, 1984), Ch.9.
12 See P. Hirst: *After Thatcher* (Collins, London, 1989).
13 S. Frith and H. Horne: *Art into pop* (Methuen ,London, 1987), p.9.
14 S. Frith: *Music for pleasure* (Polity Press, Oxford, 1988), Introduction, p.1.
15 See F. Jameson: 'Postmodernism, or the Cultural Logic of Late Capitalism' in *New left review* 146, 1984, 'The Politics of Theory' in *New german critique* 33, 1984, and 'Marxism and Postmodernism' in *New left review* 176, 1989.
16 P. Wollen: 'Ways of Thinking about Music Video (and Postmodernism)' in C. MacCabe (ed): *Future for English* (Manchester University Press, Manchester, 1988).
17 Elton John - eventually - received a settlement of £1 million from the Sun newspaper during a high court case in which the singer sued the tabloid for falsely alleging his involvement in a 'rent-boy' racket.
18 CBS Songs Ltd and others v Amstrad Consumer Electronic Plc and another, the *Times* May 13, 1988, p.21.
19 J. Baudrillard: *Forget Foucault* (Semiotext(e), New York, 1987), pp.67-69.
20 See S. Redhead: *Sing when you're winning: the last football book* (Pluto Press, London, 1987); for those who didn't get the (elaborate) joke, the book's title and format were modelled on a parody of a particular sort of (punk) pop culture mode - essentially that espoused by Julie Burchill - especially evident in a book published by Pluto Press in the late 1970s, co-authored with Tony Parsons, called *'The boy looked at Johnny': the obituary of rock and roll.*
21 C. Gillett: *The sound of the city* (Souvenir Press, London, 1983), p.255.
22 S. Frith: 'Punk is Dead, Long Live Punk' in the *Observer*, March 16, 1986.
23 The term 'post-political' has distinct meaning within the body of work

engendered by Jean Baudrillard - see S. Lotringer and C. Marazzi: 'The Return of Politics' in *Italy: Autonomia: post-political politics*, Semiotext(e), No 9, 1980. Baudrillard's notion of the 'end of' has been referred to elsewhere in this Chapter, but specifically in the context of the 'end of politics' his analysis seems to me to be 'fatally'(!) flawed. The notion of 'post-political' pop developed in this book should be seen as an attempt to find a more positive role for this concept.

Various Artists: *Bugs On The Wire* (Leghorn) was the first compilation of Sunday afternoon favourites from Steve Barker's On The Wire programme; Bruce Springsteen: *Born in the USA* (CBS); John Cougar Mellencamp: *The Lonesome Jubilee* (Mercury); The Long Ryders: 'Looking For Lewis and Clark' EP (Island); Guadalcanal Diary: *Jamboree* (Elektra); Green On Red: *Gas Food Lodging* (Zippo); Jason and the Scorchers : *Fervor* (EMI America); The Smiths: *The Queen is Dead* (Rough Trade); REM: *Murmur* and *Reckoning* (IRS); George Michael: 'Faith' (Epic) stands as an example of one lineage of New Pop clashing with the so-called New Authenticity; Human League: 'Don't You Want Me' (Virgin); Scritti Politti: *Cupid and Psyche, '85* (Virgin); Easterhouse: *Contenders* (Rough Trade); Housemartins: *London 0 Hull 4* (Go! Discs); Beastie Boys: *Licensed to Ill* (Def Jam); Prince: *Sign O The Times* and *Lovesexy* (Paisley Park) and also the *Black Album* semi-illicitly bootlegged after Prince had fallen out with WEA; Michael Jackson: *Bad* (Epic); The Judds: *Give a Little Love* (RCA); Dwight Yoakam : *Guitars, Cadillacs etc etc* and *Hillbilly Deluxe* (Reprise) ; Nanci Griffith: *The Last of the True Believers* (Rounder), and *Little Love Affairs* (MCA); Lyle Lovett: *Pontiac* and *And His Big Band* (MCA); Randy Travis: *Always and Forever* (WEA); Steve Earle: *Guitar Town* (MCA); Pogues: *Rum, Sodomy and The Lash* (Stiff), and *If I Should Fall from Grace with God* (Pogue Mahone); That Petrol Emotion: *Babble* (Polydor); a good introduction to Cooking Vinyl's roster is found on Various Artists: *Hot Cookies*; also Cowboy Junkies: *The Trinity Sessions* (Cooking Vinyl); The Christians: *The Christians* (Island); The Go Betweens: *Tallulah*(Beggars Banquet); Simple Minds: *Street Fighting Years* (Virgin); Tracy Chapman : *Tracy Chapman* (Elektra); Enya: *Watermark* (WEA); Tanita Tikaram: *Ancient Heart* (WEA); Madonna: *Like a Prayer* (Sire); Sonic Youth: *Bad Moon Rising* (Blast First); Big Dipper: *Boo Boo* (Homestead); Dead Kennedys: *Give me Convenience or give me Death* (Alternative Tentacles); Big Black: *Songs about Fucking* (Blast First);Nick Cave and the Bad Seeds: *Kicking against the Pricks* (Mute); We Free Kings: *Hell on Earth and Rosy Cross* (DDT); Gone To Earth: *Folk in Hell* and *Vegetarian Bullfigter*(Probe Plus); Camper Van Beethoven: *Camper Van Beethoven* (Rough Trade); Pet Shop Boys: *Introspective* (Parlophone); The Costello Show: *King of America* (F-Beat); Mark Stewart and the Maffia: *As the Veneer of Democracy Starts to Fade* and *Mark Stewart* (Mute); The Mekons: *New York* (Red Rhino, cassette); King of The Slums: *Barbarous English Fayre* (Play Hard); The Fall: *The Wonderful and Frightening World Of* and *The Frenz Experiment* (Beggars Banquet); Einstürzende Neubauten: *Halber Mensch* and *Five on the Open-ended Richter Scale* (Some Bizarre); Eric Clapton: *Money and Cigarettes* (WEA).

Chapter 2

1 For instance, in Nigel Fountain and Peter Everett's documentary programme for BBC Radio 4, 'The Stylographers', which was first transmitted on September 29, 1988.
2 P. Morley: *Ask; the chatter of pop* (Faber and Faber, London, 1986), p.128.
3 See I. Taylor and D. Wall: 'Beyond The Skinheads' in G. Mungham and G. Pearson (eds): *Working class youth culture* (Routledge and Kegan Paul, London, 1976).
4 From H. Chappell: 'Vault Face' in the *Guardian*, April 21, 1987.
5 See, generally, for a useful account of the Manchester design network around Factory and Manchester Polytechnic, Tim Chambers' MA Thesis, 'Leaving The Capitol: Manchester Pop Aesthetic. Graphic and Ideology, 1976-1988', Manchester Polytechnic Library.
6 L. Taylor: 'The Skin-Deep Revolution' in the *Times*, July 31, 1984.
7 J. Street: 'Red Wedge: Another Strange Story of Pop's Politics' in *Critical quarterly*, Vol 30 No 3, 1988.
8 S. Redhead and E. McLaughlin: 'Soccer's Style Wars' in *New society*, August 16, 1985,
9 See, for one such view, 'The Day The Music Died', in *New statesman and society*, February 10, 1989.
10 Quotations taken from interviews conducted with the author.
11 S. Frith: 'Introduction' to C. McGregor: *Pop goes the culture* (Pluto Press, London, 1984), p.5.
12 S. Reynolds: 'Fanzines: The Lost Moment' in *Monitor*, 1.
13 P. Cohen: 'Sore Thumb - Knuckle Sandwich Revisited' in *Youth in society*, August 1980. See also, for Phil Cohen's mid-1980s view, 'Towards Youthopia' in *Marxism today*, October 1985.
14 G. Clarke: 'Defending Ski-Jumpers: A Critique of Theories of Youth Subcultures', Centre for Contemporary Cultural Studies, Stencilled Paper, University of Birmingham, June 1982.
15 P. Willis: *Profane culture* (Routledge and Kegan Paul, London, 1978). Compare, however, Willis' work on youth for Wolverhampton Council in the 1980s, *The youth review* (Gower, Aldershot, 1988) and also 'Youth Unemployment: Ways of Living' in *New society*, April 5, 1984.
16 M. Hustwitt: 'Rocker Boy Blues' in *Screen* Vol 25 No 3, 1984. See also L. Cooke: 'Popular Culture and Rock Music' in *Screen*, Vol 24 No 3, 1983.
17. See M. Perniola: 'Time and Time Again' in *Artforum*, April 1983.
18 All quotations are from J. McDonald: 'Submission' in A. Frankovits (ed): *Seduced and abandoned: the Baudrillard scene* (Glebe, Stonemoss, 1984), pp. 24-25.
19 See on the design and musical aspects of rap and hip-hop, Joern Kroeger's undergradute graphic design thesis , 'An Illustration and Discussion of the Rise in Popularity of Rap Music', Manchester Polytechnic Library, 1988.
20 P. Virilio (with S. Lotringer): *Pure war* (Semiotext(e), New York, 1983), p.28.
21 Ibid., p.26.
22 Ibid., p.87.

23 M. Morris: 'At Henry Parkes Motel' in *Cultural studies*, Vol 2 No 1, 1988, p.3.
24 J. Berland: 'Placing Television' in *New formations*, 4, 1988, p.145.
25 Ibid., p.146. See also J. Berland: 'Locating Listening' in *Cultural studies*, Vol 2 No 3, 1988.

Fields of the Nephilim: *Dawn Razor* (Situation Two); The Mission: *Children* (Mercury); New Order: *Low-Life, Brotherhood, Substance*, and *Technique* (Factory); The Smiths: *Strangeways Here we Come* (Rough Trade); Half Man, Half Biscuit: *Back in the DHSS* and *Back in the DHSS Again* (Probe Plus); I, Ludicrous: 'Quite Extraordinary' and *Its Like Everything Else* (Kaleidoscope); Frank Sidebottom: 5:9:88 (In Tape); Latin Quarter: *Modern Times* (A&M); A Certain Ratio: *Force* (Factory); Happy Mondays: *Squirrel and G-Man ...*, and *Bummed* (Factory); Schoolly-D : *Schoolly-D* (Flame) is a good example of the macho 'braggard' hip-hop school; Cookie Crew: 'Females' (Serious) and Salt'n'Papa: 'Push It' (Champion) are instances of female rap crews' response; also, for the development of rap and hip-hop: Spoonie Gee: 'The Godfather/Sure Delight' (Tuff City), Eric B and Rakim: 'I Know You Got Soul' (Cooltempo) and 'Paid in Full (Cold Cut Re-Mix)' (4th and Broadway), Public Enemy: 'Public Enemy No 1' (Def Jam); Mantronix: *Music Madness* (10); MC Buzz B: 'Slap Head' (Play Hard); also good hip-hop collections can be found on: *Hip-hop, 20* (StreetSounds), Various Artists: *The Word is Rap* (Jive) including the Skinny Boys; Various Artists: *The Best of West Coast Hip hop* (StreetSounds), featuring Ice T amongst others ; Various Artists: *Beat the Freaks* (Celluloid) which includes the classic original rappers The Last Poets and even New York avant-'rockers' the Golden Palominos; and Various Artists: *The B-Boy/Boogie Down Sampler Vol 2* (Westside), including KRS-One and Cold Crush Brothers on a celebration of two of New York's best known rap labels; for house compilations *House Sound of Chicago Vol 1, 2 and 3* (ffrr), the latter being one of the earliest to focus on 'Acid'; for the best instances of Acid House, Various Artists: *Acido Amigo* (Westside) featuring Tyree, Jack Rabbit (aka Adonis) and Humanoid who had a chart single 'Stakker Humanoid'; DJ Fast Eddie's 'hip-house' mixture is best heard on *Jack to the Sound* (DJ International); T-Coy: 'Carino' (De/Construction) is house straight from the Hacienda's mouth.

Chapter 3

1 M. Omi: 'A Positive Noise: The Charity Rock Phenomenon' in *Socialist review* no 86, 1986, p. 111.
2 S. Connor: 'The Flag on the Road' in *New formations*, 3, 1987 and S. Connor: *Postmodernist culture* (Blackwell, Oxford, 1989).
3 M. Kohn: 'Hip Little Englanders' in *Marxism today*, November 1983.
4 M. Harron: 'No One's Fault' in *New statesman*, November 19, 1982.
5 A. Martin and G. Hayes, op. cit., p. 164.
6 See S. Frith: 'Frankie Says Buy Me' in *Onetwothreefour*, no 2, 1985.
7 J. Baudrillard: *The evil demon of images* (Power Institute of Fine Art, Sydney, 1987), p. 16.

8 For a critical study of this term as developed by theorists such as Antonio Gramsci, see D. Forgacs: 'National-Popular: the Genealogy of a Concept' in T. Bennett et al (eds): *Formations: of nation and people* (Routledge and Kegan Paul, London, 1984).
9 I. A. Anderson: 'Editorial' in *Folk roots*, June 1986.
10 I. A. Anderson: 'A World Music Meeting' in *Folk roots*, July 1986.
11 R. Denselow: 'Folk-Rock in Britain' in D. Laing et al: *The electric muse* (Eyre Methuen, London, 1975).
12 Interview on 'Saturday Live' on BBC Radio 1, April 27, 1985.
13 S. Frith: 'Rock Goes back to the Real Stuff' in the *Observer*, May 6, 1985.
14 I. A. Anderson: 'Editorial' in *Folk roots*, August 1986.
15 Interview with the author.
16 Interview in *City life*, April 5-26, 1984.
17 Interview with the author.
18 The programme on Ry Cooder was broadcast on February 27, 1983, and presented by the late Alexis Korner. See also the book of the series, edited by John Tobler and Stuart Grundy, *The guitar greats* (BBC Publications, London, 1983).
19 M. Kohn: *Narcomania* (Faber and Faber, London, 1987), p. 168.
20 F. Jameson: 'Postmodernism and Consumer Society' in H. Foster (ed), *Postmodern culture* (Pluto Press, London, 1985).
21 Interview with the author.
22 See J. Walker: *Cross-overs* (Comedia/Methuen, London, 1987).
23 S. Frith: *Sound effects* op. cit., p. 29.
24 D. Hebdige: *Subculture: the meaning of style* (Methuen, London, 1979).
25 D. Hebdige: *Cut 'n' mix* (Comedia/Methuen, 1987), p. 158.
26 R. Davis: 'Anti-Pop but not Iggy Pop' in *Left curve*, no 12, 1987-8.
27 J. Murphy: 'Interview with Fredric Jameson' in *Left curve*, no 12, 1987-8, p. 11.
28 Ibid., p. 11.
29 Editorial, *Left curve*, no 12, 1987-8.
30 L. Hutcheon: *A poetics of postmodernism* (Routledge, London, 1988), p. 60.
31 Ibid., p. 61.
32 Ibid., p. 67.
33 Quotations taken from interviews with the author.

Michael Chapman: *Heartbeat* (Coda); Incantation: *Panpipes of the Andes* (Coda); Claire Hamill: *Love in the afternoon* (Coda); Various Artists: *First Impressions* (Coda); Robert Cray Band: *Bad Influence* and *False Accusations* (Demon); Anita Baker: *The Songstress*, *Rapture* and *Giving you the best that I Got* (Elektra); Luther Vandross: *Give me the Reason* (Epic); Melis'a Morgan: *Do Me Baby* (Capitol); Bruce Springsteen: *Live 1975-1985* (5 album boxed set, CBS); Frankie Goes to Hollywood: *Welcome to the Pleasure Dome* (ZTT); Ketama: *Ketama* (Hannibal); Les Mystere Des Voix Bulgares: *Vol 2* (4AD); Balkana: *The Music of Bulgaria* (Hannibal); Marta Sebestyen and Muzsikas: *Marta Sebestyen* (Hannibal); 3 Mustaphas 3: *Bam! Mustaphas Play Stereo* (GlobeStyle); Bhundu Boys: *True Jit* (WEA); Ali Farka Toure: *Ali Farka Toure* (World Circuit); Stella

Chiweshe: *Ambuya?* (GlobeStyle); Toumani Diabate: *Kaira* (Hannibal); Jali Musa Jawara: *Soubindoor* (World Circuit); Salif Keita: *Soro*(Sterns); The Real Sounds: *Wende Zako* (Cooking Vinyl); *Various Artists: Thunder Before the Dawn: The Indestructible Beat of Soweto, Vol 2* (Earthworks/Virgin); The Oyster Band: *Wide Blue Yonder*(Cooking Vinyl); Band of Holy Joy: 'Rosemary Smith' (Flim Flam); for a Billy Bragg 'soundalike' who encountered the same problems see Rodney Allen: *Happysad* (Subway); Sweet Honey in The Rock: *The Other Side* (Making Waves); The Sugarcubes: 'Birthday', 'Deus' and 'Cold Sweat' (One Little Indian); Throwing Muses: *Throwing Muses*, 'Chains Changed' EP, *The Fat Skier* and *House Tornado* (4AD); Golden Palominos: *Visions of Excess* (Celluloid); 10,000 Maniacs: *Human Conflict No 5* and *Blind Man's Zoo* (Elektra); Rory McLeod: *Angry Love* (Forward); The Proclaimers: *This is the Story* (Chrysalis); Richard Thompson: *Amnesia* (Capitol); The Men They Couldn't Hang: 'Gold Rush/The Ghosts of Cable Street' (MCA) and *Night of a Thousand Candles* (Imp); Dick Gaughan: *True and Bold* (STUC); Christy Moore: *Unfinished Revolution* (WEA) ; Michelle Shocked: *Short Sharp Shocked* (Cooking Vinyl); Phranc: *Folksinger* (Stiff); Loudon Wainwright III: *More Love Songs*(Demon); Jackson Browne: *Lives in the Balance* (Geffen); Joni Mitchell: *Dog Eat Dog* (Geffen); Andy White: *Rave On* (Decca); Felt: *Forever Breathes the Lonely Word* (Creation); Peter Case: *The Man with the Blue Postmodern Fragmented Neo-Traditionalist Guitar* (Geffen); Martin Stephenson and the Daintees: *Boat to Bolivia* (Kitchenware); Leonard Cohen: *I'm Your Man* (CBS); Prefab Sprout: *Swoon*, *Steve McQueen*,*From Langley Park to Memphis* and *Protest Songs* (Kitchenware); Terry Allen: *Bloodlines* (Making Waves); Rhythm Sisters: *Road to Roundhay Pier* (Red Rhino); Paul Simon: *Graceland* (WEA); Ted Hawkins: *On the Boardwalk* (UnAmerican Activities); S.E.Rogie: *Palm Wine Guitar Music* (Cooking Vinyl); Clive Gregson: *Strange Persuasions* (Demon); Ry Cooder: 'Get Rhythm' (WEA); Los Lobos: *How Will The Wolf Survive?* (Slash/London); Jesus and Mary Chain: 'April Skies' (Blanco Y Negro); The Bodines: 'Therese' (Creation); The Pastels: *Up for a Bit With* (Glass); Primal Scream: *Sonic Flower Groove* (Elevation); That Petrol Emotion: *Manic Pop Thrill* (Polydor); Any Trouble: *Wrong End of the Race* (EMI America); The Soup Dragons: 'Whole Wide World' (Subway); Razorcuts: 'Sorry To Embarass You' (Subway); Shop Assistants: *Shop Assistants* (Blue Guitar); Ofra Haza: 'Im Nin' Alu', and *Yemenite Songs* (GlobeStyle); Van Morrison and The Chieftains: *Irish Heartbeat* (Mercury); Relativity: *Relativity* (Green Linnet); Heb Gariad: 'Caneuon O' R De' (Anhrefn); also *Keltia-Rok* (Sain), which was the first record to bring together rock music in the 6 Celtic languages (Welsh, Cornish, Breton, Irish, Manx, Scottish Gaelic); The Chills: *Brave Words* (Flying Nun); for reverential post-punk Johnny Cash, Various Artists: *Til Things Get Brighter* (Red Rhino).

Chapter 4

1 D. Hebdige: *Subculture; the meaning of style*, op. cit., p.148.
2 J. Savage: 'Dead Souls' in *New Statesman*, February 6, 1987.
3 Quoted in *Melody Maker*, March 28, 1987.
4 See S. Hall: 'The Hippies: An American Moment' (Stencilled paper, Centre

for Contemporary Cultural Studies, University of Birmingham, 1968).

5 J. Savage: 'Dead Souls', op.cit. See also P. Vincent-Jones: 'Private Property and Public Order: the 'Hippy Convoy' and Criminal Trespass' in *Journal of law and society*, Vol 13 No 3, 1986 and M. Clarke: *The politics of pop festivals* (Junction Books, London, 1982).

6 R. Hewison: *Too much* (Methuen, London, 1986), p.xi.

7 R. Duncan: *The noise: notes from a rock'n'roll era* (Ticknor and Fields, New York, 1984), p. 11.

8 Quoted in R. Woliver: *Bringing it all back home* (Pantheon, New York, 1986), p. 31.

9 P. York: *Style wars* (Sidgwick and Jackson, London, 1980), p.182. The Chapter was originally published in *Harpers and queen*, January 1978.

10 G. Marcus: 'Speaker to Speaker' column *Artforum*, March 1987.

11 See B. Dessau: 'Shamble City' in *City limits*, April 17-24, 1986.

12 S. Reynolds: 'MOR Or Less' in *New statesman* December 19/26, 1986. See also Reynolds' other excellent pieces on shambling - 'Younger than Yesterday' in *Melody maker*, June 28, 1986, 'Ladybirds and Start Rite-Kids' in *Melody maker*, September 27, 1986, and his article on Talulah Gosh in *Melody maker*, November 13, 1986.

13 S. Frith: 'Punk is Dead, Long Live Punk' op. cit.

14 i-D no 46, 1987.

15 S. Frith: 'The Punk Bohemians' in *New society*, March 9, 1978, my emphasis.

16 M. Middles: *The Smiths* (Omnibus, London, 1985), p. 38.

17 Quotation from interviews with Dave Haslam by the author. One of the earliest and most revealing interviews with Morrissey was conducted by Dave Haslam and appeared in *Debris* issue 2 in 1984. Haslam argued in the preface that Morrissey's 'heroines of the 60's (Sandie Shaw, Dusty Springfield) might seem to be unashamedly innocent and honestly charming in what they do, but that whole image was as much a marketing ploy as any in use in today's music business.'

18 P. Willis: 'Young, Gifted and Forgotten' in *New socialist*, Summer 1988.

19 J. Attali: *Noise: the political economy of music* (Manchester University Press, Manchester, 1985)

MC Buzz B: 'How Sleep The Brave' (Play Hard); Benny Profane: *Trapdoor Swing* (Play Hard); The Bodines: 'Decide' (Play Hard); The Train Set: 'She's Gone', and 'Hold On' (Play Hard); much hardcore 'punk' and 'rock', and thrash, speed and even death 'metal', takes on the two traditions , punk and hippy, in its three chord hi-velocity thrash and its long-hair styles - for British examples, Doom: *War Crimes: Inhuman Beings* (Peaceville), Toranga: *Bastard Ballads* (Peaceville); Deviated Instinct: *Rock'n'Roll Conformity* (Peaceville); Gold, Frankincense and Disk Drive: *Where do we Draw the Line* (Peaceville); Gaye Bikers on Acid: *Drill Your Own Hole* (In Tape), and Various Artists: *A Vile Peace* (Peaceville); Hüsker Dü: *Candy Apple Grey* (SST) and *Warehouse: Songs and Stories* (WEA) are still probably the outstanding examples from either side of the mid-Atlantic; for North American punk, 'hardcore' and beyond in the wake of Hüsker Dü's first album *Land Speed Record*

(New Alliance/SST), play also: Black Flag : *Damaged* (SST) featuring the vocals of Henry Rollins; Blast: *Its in My Blood* (SST); The Jesus Lizard: *Pure* (Touch and Go); The Descendents: *Two Things at Once* (SST); The Didjits: *Hey Judester* (Touch and Go); Die Kreuzen: 'Gone Away', and *Century Days* (Touch and Go); Laughing Hyenas: *Merry Go Round* (Touch and Go) ; Pailhead: *Trait* (Wax Trax); Flour: *Flour* (Touch and Go); Fire Party: *Fire Party* and *New Orleans Opera* (Dischord); Killdozer: 'Lupus/ Nasty' (Touch and Go); SNFU: *Better Than a Stick in the Eye* (Cargo); and Various Artists: *The New Sound Of Rock* (Celluloid); though this is mostly a 'white' musical form there are exceptions like the all black band Bad Brains: *I Against I* (SST); though this is usually a genre best exemplified by American bands, play Silverfish: 'Silverfish' EP (Wiiija) and Bastard Kestrel: *Oh Stupid Mushroom* (Wiiija); The Cult: *Electric*, and *Love* (Beggars Banquet) relied on less punk, some Goth and a more traditional combination of 1960s and 1970s rock styles; for up to the minute accounts of bands and labels - like Seattle's Sub Pop - see the US magazine *Maximium rock and roll*; from another perspective altogether, Black Sun Ensemble: *Black Sun Ensemble* (Reckless) revive a style and sound from the late 1960s wholesale; for an example of the 'new jazz' see Courtney Pine: *Destiny's Song and the Image of Pursuance* (Antilles/Island); for one version of British 'indie' pop of the mid-late 1980s: The Woodentops: Giant (Rough Trade); The Rosehips: 'Room in Your Heart', and 'I Shouldn't Have To Say' (Subway); Talulah Gosh: 'Steaming Train' (53rd and 3rd); The Primitives: 'Stop Killing Me' (Lazy); The Flatmates: 'Shimmer', 'You're Gonna Cry' and 'Happy All the Time'(Subway); and The Chesterfields: *Westward Ho* and *Kettle* (Subway); for Morrissey post-Smiths, but with Durutti Column's Vini Reilly: *Viva Hate* (HMV); for sub/post Smiths shambling guitar bands: The Wedding Present: 'Why Are You Being So Reasonable Now?' (Reception); The Railway Children: *Reunion Wilderness* (Factory); Bradford: 'Skin Storm' (Village); Various Artists: *The Edge of the Road* (Medium Cool) featuring the Waltones and Corn Dollies; and The Waltones: 'Spell It Out' (Medium Cool); for less irony and more straightforward reworking of pop and rock tradition: Inspiral Carpets: *The Peel Sessions* (Strange Fruit) and The Stone Roses: *The Stone Roses* (Silvertone); for 'left-field' bands in the mould of a mixture of Big Flame and Captain Beefheart see: Dub Sex: *Push* (Ugly Man,) and 'The Underneath' (Cut Deep); and Death By Milkfloat: 'The Absolute Non-End' EP (Ediesta); for the sound of 'white' American new bohemia, Pere Ubu: *The Tenement Year* (Fontana); The Pixies: *Surfer Rosa* (4AD); Swans: 'Time is Money (Bastard)' (K422) and *This Burning World* (MCA).

Chapter 5

1 See I. Chambers: 'Maps For the Metropolis: A Possible Guide to the Present' in *Cultural studies* Vol 1 No 1, 1987, and 'Contamination, Coincidence and Collusion: Pop Music, Urban Culture and the Avant-Garde' in L. Grossberg and C. Nelson (eds): *Marxism and the interpretation of culture* (University of Illinois Press, Urbana, 1988); and D. Hebdige: 'The Impossible Object: Towards a Sociology of the Sublime' in *New formations*, 1, 1987.

2 J. McDonald: 'Submission' op. cit., p23.
3 R. Harley: 'Hiding in the Light: Extended Club Mix With Dick Hebdige' in *Art and text*, no 26, 1987, p.70.
4 See A. Chester: 'For A Rock Aesthetic' in *New left review*, 59, 1970, R. Merton: 'Comment' in *New left review*, 1970, A. Chester: 'Second Thoughts on a Rock Aesthetic' in *New left review*, 62, 1970, and S. Frith: 'Towards An Aesthetic of Popular Music' in R. Leppert and S. McClary (eds): *Music and society* (Cambridge University Press, Cambridge, 1987).
5 A. Durant: *Conditions of music* (Macmillan, London, 1984), Ch. 6.
6 S. Frith: 'Art Theory and Pop Practice' in L. Grossberg and C. Nelson (eds), op. cit.
7 J. Burchill: 'Adorno and Rice' in *New society*, December 18, 1987.
8 S. Frith: 'Why Do Songs Have Words?' in A. L. White (ed): *Lost in music*, Sociological review monograph, University of Keele, 34 (Routledge, London, 1987).
9 Interviews with the author.
10 See J. Dawe: 'Relationship Between Experimental "Rock" Music and Experimental "Art" Music', undergraduate Fine Art thesis, Humberside College of Higher Education, 1988.
11 Interviews with the author.

Sonic Youth: *Daydream Nation* (Blast First); Various Artists: *Funky Alternatives* (Concrete); African Head Charge: *Off the Beaten Track* and *Environmental Studies* (On-U Sound); Singers and Players: *Staggering Heights* and *Vacuum Pumping* (On-U Sound); Gary Clail's Tackhead Sound System: *Tackhead Tape Time* (Nettwerk); Tackhead: *Friendly as a Hand Grenade* (World Records); Lee 'Scratch' Perry and Dub Syndicate: *Time Boom X de Devil Dead* (EMI); Dub Organiser: 'I've Got A Weapon' (Play Hard); What?noise: 'Vein' EP (Cut Deep); Thule: 'Le Jamais Contente' EP (Wiiija); The Shamen: 'Jesus Loves Amerika' (Ediesta); Gang of Four: *The Peel Sessions* (Strange Fruit); Run DMC: *Tougher Than Leather* (Profile); Public Enemy: *It Takes a Nation of Millions to Hold us Back* (Def Jam); Cold Cut: 'Doctorin The House' (Ahead of Our Time); Eric B and Rakim: *Follow The Leader* (MCA); S-Express: 'Theme From S-Express' (Rhythm King); Bomb The Bass: 'Enter The Dragon' (Rhythm King); Yazz: 'Fine Time' (Big Life); for much litigated sampling, Justified Ancients of Mu Mu: *Who Killed the JAMS?* (KLF); for all-women reggae, Akabu: Akabu (Viva).

The absolute non-end

1 For a stimulating debate on the reformulation of the authentic/inauthentic dichotomy see L. Grossberg et al: *Its a sin* (Power Publications, Sydney, 1988).

Guide to further reading

This is a selected guide to further reading on the themes of the book. Most pop books are 'bio-pics'. I have drawn on them only where strictly necessary. The fanzines/magazines I have used are mainly referenced in the text. However, I do strongly recommend back issues of *Monitor*, *Collusion* and *Debris*.

Pop history/rock theory

Simon Frith and Howard Horne: *Art into pop* (Methuen, London, 1987) especially Ch. 1 and 5, contains excellent summary and critique of 'postmodernism and pop'. The best article I have read on the subject is Andrew Goodwin: 'Sample and Hold: Pop Music in The Digital Age of Reproduction' in *Critical quarterly*, Vol 30 No 3, 1988. See also, Jon Stratton: 'Beyond Art : Postmodernism and the Case of Popular Music' in *Theory, culture and society*, Vol 6 No 1, 1989 and Lawrence Grossberg: 'The Politics of Youth Culture' in *Social text*, 8, 1984, 'I'd Rather Feel Bad Than Not Feel Anything At All' in *enclitic*, 8, 1984, and 'The Politics of Music' in *Canadian journal of political and social theory*, 11, 1987. For a different trajectory, see Dick Hebdige: *Hiding in the light: on images and things* (Comedia, London, 1988). Dave Harker: *One for the money* (Hutchinson, London, 1980), David Widgery: *Beating time* (Chatto and Windus, London, 1986), John Street: *Rebel rock* (Basil Blackwell, Oxford, 1986) and Robin Denselow: *When the music's over: the story of political pop* (Faber and Faber, London, 1989) are differing ways of viewing rock's potential for rebellion and resistance. Dave Marsh: *Before I get old: the story of The Who* (Plexus, London, 1983) and *Glory days: a biography of Bruce Springsteen* (Sidgwick and Jackson, London, 1987) – which is a sequel to *Born to run : the Bruce Springsteen story* (Omnibus, London, 1981) – give a specific interpretation of his particular pop heroes in accordance with one theory of the rock ethos. Marsh's US monthly newsletter *Rock and roll confidential* performs this function on a regular basis. From a different perspective on the USA, Greil Marcus: *Mystery train* (E.p. Dutton, New York, 1982) is still a fascinating read, while his *Lipstick Traces* (Secker and Warburg, London, 1989) is confirmation of the importance of Dada as counter-culture in pop history. Simon Garfield: *Expensive habits* (Faber and Faber, London, 1986) and John Qualen: *The music industry: the end of vinyl?* (Comedia, London, 1985) consider, critically, different aspects of the music industry, as does Roger Wallis and Krister Malm: *Big sounds from small peoples* (Constable, London, 1984). James Lull (ed): *Popular music and communication* (Sage, London and Beverly Hills, 1987) collects together a number of essays on these and other themes. Jon Wiener: *Come together:*

John Lennon in his time (Faber and Faber, London, 1985), Philip Norman: *The Stones* (Elm Tree, London, 1984), Philip Norman: *Shout! : the true story of The Beatles* (Corgi, London, 1982), Richard DiLello: *The longest cocktail party* (Charisma, London, 1973) and Eric Burdon: *I used to be an Animal but I'm all right now* (Faber and Faber, London, 1987) all help to dissect 1960s rock myths. On the 1970s and early 1980s, see Philip Norman: *The road goes on forever* (Corgi, London, 1982). Fred and Judy Vermorel: *Starlust: the secret life of fans* (Comet, London, 1985) explodes the myth of pop fans as passive, exploited consumers. As a reference book first published in 1970, Charlie Gillett: *The sound of the city: the rise of rock and roll* (revised edition, Souvenir Press, London, 1983) is exemplary for the period up to the early 1970s. For a more recent contrast, see Ed Ward et al: *Rock of ages: the Rolling Stone history of rock and roll* (Penguin, Harmondsworth, 1986). Nik Cohn: *AwopBopaLooBopLopBam-Boom: pop from the beginning* (Paladin, London,1970) is a landmark; see, too, the collection *Ball the wall : Nik Cohn in the age of Rock* (Pan, London, 1989) with an introduction by Gordon Burn. For a comparison with Cohn's British pop theory, see Richard Meltzer: *The aesthetics of rock* (Da Capo, New York, 1987), with a new and enlightening introduction by Greil Marcus, originally published in 1970 in the USA. For papers generated within the International Association For the Study of Popular Music (IASPM), see David Horn (ed): *Popular music perspectives, 2* (IASPM, Gothenburg, Reggio, Exeter, 1985) and Simon Frith (ed): *World music, politics and social change* (Manchester University Press, Manchester, 1989).

Pop and sexuality

See, for the important debate which still sets the terms today, Simon Frith and Angela McRobbie: 'Rock and Sexuality' in *Screen education*, 29, 1979 and the response by Dave Laing and Jenny Taylor: 'Disco-Pleasure-Discourse' in *Screen education*, 31, 1979. See also, various essays in Simon Frith: *Music for pleasure* (Polity Press, Oxford, 1988), and the contributions by Suzanne Moore and Frank Mort to Rowena Chapman and Jonathan Rutherford (eds): *Male order: unwrapping masculinity* (Lawrence and Wishart, London, 1988). For Michel Foucault's notion of the history of sexuality which I have used in this book, see *The history of sexuality. Volume 1: an introduction* (Allen Lane, London, 1979) and *The use of pleasure. Volume 2: the history of sexuality* (Penguin, Harmondsworth, 1987).

Pop and gender

Sue Steward and Sheryl Garratt: *Signed, sealed and delivered: true life stories of women in pop* (Pluto Press, London, 1984) is excellent. Also, see Robyn Archer and Diana Simmonds: *A star is torn* (Virago, London, 1986) and Wilfrid Mellers: *Angels in the night* (Faber and Faber, London, 1986). *Womens revolutions per minute (WRPM)* catalogue is available from 62, Woodstock Road, Birmingham B13 9BN.

Pop and race

David Toop: *The rap attack: African jive to New York hip hop* (Pluto Press, London, 1984), Dick Hebdige: *Cut 'n' mix: culture, identity and Caribbean music* (Comedia, London, 1987), Simon Jones: *Black culture, white youth* (Macmillan, London, 1988) and Paul Gilroy: *There ain't no black in the Union Jack* (Hutchinson, London, 1987), especially Chapter 5, are all essential reading. See also Paul Giroy's contributions to the Centre for Contemporary Cultural Studies: *The empire strikes back* (Hutchinson, London, 1982), and Paul Gilroy and Errol Lawrence: 'Two Tone Britain' in Phil Cohen and Harwant Bains (eds): *Multi-racist Britain* (Macmillan, London, 1988).

New pop

Dave Rimmer: *Like punk never happened: Culture Club and the new pop* (Faber and Faber, London, 1985), Dave Hill: *Designer boys and material girls* (Blandford Press, Poole, 1986) and Bob Geldof: *Is that it?* (Sidgwick and Jackson, London, 1986) all tell the story of New Pop's rise and fall, from different perspectives. Its most prominent theorist, Paul Morley, finally buries it in *Ask: the chatter of pop* (Faber and Faber, London, 1986). On one band which emerged from its wings claiming a very different rock heritage, see Eamon Dunphy: *Unforgettable fire: the story of U2* (Viking, London, 1987).

Punk

Dave Laing: *One chord wonders: power and meaning in punk rock* (Open University Press, Milton Keynes, 1985) mixes semiotics, Souxsie, and the Sex Pistols with ease. Jon Savage and Jamie Reid: *Up they rise: the incomparable works of Jamie Reid* (Faber and Faber, London, 1987), Fred and Judy Vermorel: *The Sex Pistols* (third edition, Omnibus, London, 1987), Caroline Coon: *1988: The New Wave punk rock explosion* (Omnibus, London, 1982), and Tony Parsons and Julie Burchill: *'The boy looked at Johnny': the obituary of rock and roll* (Pluto Press, London, 1978) all try to tell it how it was.

Folk/roots

Dave Harker: *Fakesong* (Open University Press, Milton Keynes, 1986) imposes an historical materialist grid over the 'manufacture' of folk song since the eighteenth century. Robin Denselow, Karl Dallas, Dave Laing and Robert Shelton: *The electric muse: the story of folk into rock* (Methuen, London, 1975) accompanied a four album record of the state of folk/rock by the mid-1970s. Robbie Woliver: *Bringing it all back home: twenty-five years of American music at Folk City* (Pantheon, New York, 1986) celebrates one of New York's most famous venues. Robert Shelton: *No direction home: the life and music of Bob Dylan* (New English Library, London, 1986) is the mammoth biography that could have been published any time from the late 1960s onwards. Michael Gray: *The art of Bob Dylan* (Hamlyn, London, 1981) is a revised edition of *Song and dance man: the art of Bob Dylan* (Hart-Davis, McGibbon, London, 1972). Gray has also edited a collection of pieces from the first 25 issues of the Dylan fanzine, *The telegraph*, with its editor, John Bauldie: *All across the telegraph: a Bob Dylan handbook* (Sidgwick and Jackson, London, 1987). Magazines such as *Folk roots* (formerly *Southern rag*) and *Swing 51* have also documented, and indeed defined, 'roots' music. Most significantly, *Folk roots* has helped to champion African music; on which see Ronnie Graham: *Stern's guide to contemporary African music* (Zwan, London, 1988).

Subculture/youth culture theory

Dick Hebdige: *Subculture: the meaning of style* (Methuen, London, 1979) is quite rightly still being reprinted almost annually. Iain Chambers: *Urban rhythms* (Macmillan, London, 1985) and *Popular culture: the metropolitan experience* (Methuen, London, 1986) explore pop consumption. Simon Frith: *Sound effects* (Constable, London, 1983) is a completely revised version of *The sociology of rock* (Constable, London, 1978). See also, Simon Frith: *The sociology of youth* (Causeway, Ormskirk, 1984), John Muncie: *'The trouble with kids today'* (Hutchinson, London, 1984) especially Ch. 4 and 5, and Mike Brake: *Comparative youth culture* (Routledge and Kegan Paul, London, 1985) which is an updated and extended version of his *Sociology of youth culture and youth subcultures* (Routledge and Kegan Paul, London, 1980). For 1970s subcultural work see: Stuart Hall and Tony Jefferson (eds): *Resistance through rituals* (Hutchinson, London, 1978) originally a special issue, no. 7/8, of *Working papers in cultural studies* published by the Centre for Contemporary Cultural Studies at the University of Birmingham; Paul Willis: *Profane culture* (Routledge and Kegan Paul, London, 1978) and Paul Willis: *Learning to labour* (Saxon House, Farnborough, 1977); Phil Cohen and David Robins: *Knuckle sandwich* (Penguin, London, 1978). For a quite different viewpoint, see Stan Cohen: *Folk devils and moral panics* (Blackwell, Oxford, 1987) which is a reprinting of the second edition – with the important new 'Introduction' – published by Martin Robertson in 1980; the book was first published in 1972. For other work which develops and criticises the CCCS tradition, see: Nick Dorn and Nigel South: *Of males and markets* (Centre For Occupational and Community Research, Middlesex Polytechnic, 1982), Angela McRobbie and Mica Nava (eds): *Gender and generation* (Macmillan, London, 1984), Elizabeth Wilson: *Adorned in dreams: fashion and modernity* (Virago, London, 1985), and Phil Cohen et al: *Schooling for the dole* (Macmillan, London, 1984). Peter Everett: *You'll never be sixteen again* (BBC Publications, London, 1986) is a useful accompaniment to the BBC Radio 4 series of the same name transmitted in 1985, and expanded for transmission on BBC Radio 1 in 1986. Stuart Cosgrove: 'The Zoot-Suit and Style Warfare' in *History workshop*, 18, 1984, Steve Chibnall: 'Whistle and Zoot: The Changing Meaning of a Suit of Clothes' in *History workshop*, 20, 1985, and Steve Chibnall: 'Ere Lady, Wanna Buy Some Nylons' in *New society*, December 20/27, 1984, are all useful 'archaeologies' of hidden youth styles.

Pop fiction

As with his pop theory book, Nik Cohn: *I'm still the greatest says Johnny Angelo* (Penguin, Harmondsworth, 1970) – originally published in 1967 – sets the standard for the 'pop culture' novel. Colin MacInnes: *Absolute beginners* (Allison and Busby, London, 1980, first published in 1959) comes a close second. The 1980s 'life-stylists' are refracted through Jay McInerney: *Bright lights, big city* (Jonathan Cape, London, 1985), Bret Easton Ellis: *Less than zero* (Pan, London, 1986), and Michael Bracewell: *The crypto-amnesia club* (Serpent's Tail, London, 1988). Pete Davies: *The last election* (Penguin, Harmondsworth, 1987) gives this genre a harder, more cutting, political edge. The funniest books in this vein, though still lacking punch, are Martin Millar: *Milk, sulphate and Alby Starvation*, (Fourth Estate London, 1987), Martin Millar: *Lux the poet* (Fourth Estate, London, 1988) and *Ruby and the stone age diet* (Fourth Estate, London, 1989). The 1970s skinhead, crombie and punk styles are the basis for Richard Allen's paperback pulp novels: see, for instance, *Suedehead* (New English Library, London, 1971) in a series which has now achieved the dubious honour of cult status – in other words you have to pay £3.50 for a copy of *Punk Rock*, *Sorts*, *Smoothies*, *Boot Boys*, or *Skinhead* in the second-hand shops! In many ways though, the more successful fiction in this field has been from those who are writers first and pop fans second: see, Philip Norman: *Wild thing* (Dent, London, 1983), Roddy Doyle: *The commitments* (Heinemann, London, 1988), and Bobbie Ann Mason: *In country* (Flamingo, London, 1987). Iain Banks: *Espedair street* (Macmillan, London, 1987) and Tony Parsons: *Platinum logic* (Pan, London, 1981) don't quite fulfill their initial promise. Robert Elms shows how not to do it in *In search of the crack* (Penguin, Harmondsworth, 1989).The first 1990s pulp novel is Trevor Miller: *Trip city* (Avernus, London, 1989), complete with good soundtrack by A Guy Called Gerald.

Pop and style

The 1980s focus on design and visual style is illustrated profusely in Jon Wozencroft and Neville Brody: *The graphic language of Neville Brody* (Thames and Hudson, London, 1988). Catherine McDermott: *Street style: British design in the 1980s* (Design Council, London, 1987) looks at the notion of 'youth culture' as a design tradition, though the book is marred by the lack of proof-reading in the otherwise useful bibliography. Peter York: *Style wars* (Sidgwick and Jackson, London, 1980) and *Modern times* (Heinemann, London, 1984) trace a journalistic career which has become progressively more self-parodic; as do Julie Burchill: *Love it or shove it* (Century, London, 1985) and *Damaged gods: cults and heroes reappraised* (Century, London, 1986). Picture books of 'youth styles' abound; see Maz Harris: *Bikers* (Faber and Faber, London, 1985), Johnny Stuart: *Rockers!* (Plexus, London, 1987), Mick Farren: *The Black Leather Jacket* (Plexus, London, 1985), Nick Knight: *Skinhead* (Omnibus, London, 1982), Richard Barnes: *Mods* (Eel Pie, London, 1979), Chris Steele-Perkins and Richard Smith: *The Teds* (second edition, Travelling Light/Exit, 1987). Also, i-D's Christmas special for 1987, *The i-D bible: every ultimate victim's handbook* and i-D no 46, 1987 provided late 1980s updates. Roy

Carr, Brian Case and Fred Dellar: *The hip: hipsters, jazz and the beat generation* (Faber and Faber, London, 1986) rewinds jazz styles in history just as they became fashionable again. The magazines, *Wire* and *Straight no chaser*, testify to the broadening definitions of 'jazz' styles. Writing style, though, remains pop's most lasting contribution: for three completely contrasting collections, see Lester Bangs: *Psychotic reactions and carburettor dung* (Knopf, New York, 1988), Dave Marsh: *Fortunate son* (Random House, New York, 1985), and Craig McGregor: *Pop goes the culture* (Pluto Press, London, 1984), with an introduction by Simon Frith.

Pop mythologies

For rock'n'roll myth-making see: Chuck Berry: *The autobiography* (Faber and Faber, London, 1988) and Charles White: *The life and times of Little Richard* (Pan, London, 1985). For soul myths and their deconstruction, see the magazine *Soul underground*, Gerri Hirschey: *Nowhere to run* (Pan, London, 1985), Barney Hoskyns: *Say it one time for the broken-hearted* (Fontana, London, 1987), Peter Guralnick: *Sweet soul music* (Harper and Row, New York, 1986), Ian Hoare (ed): *The soul book* (Eyre Methuen, London, 1975), and Bruce Tucker, with James Brown: *James Brown: the godfather of soul* (Fontana, London, 1988). On Motown, see Nelson George: *Where did our love go* (Omnibus, London, 1986). On country and blues, see: Peter Guralnick: *Lost highway* (Vintage, New York, 1982), and Bob Brunning: *Blues: the British connection* (Blandford Press, Poole, 1986). On punk, post-punk and 'avant-noise' see Charles Neal: *Tape delay* (SAF, London, 1987) and M.Fish and D.Hallberry: *Cabaret Voltaire: the art of the sixth sense* (2nd edition, SAF, London, 1989).

Pop and media

On radio, Stephen Barnard: *On the radio* (Open University Press, Milton Keynes, 1988), and John Hind and Stephen Mosco: *Rebel radio: the full story of British pirate radio* (Pluto Press, London, 1985). On film, see Fred Dellar: *The NME guide to rock cinema* (Hamlyn, London, 1981). On pop video, E. Ann Kaplan: *Rocking around the clock* (Methuen, London, 1987) is a problematic reading of MTV; see also Mark Hustwitt: 'Sure Feels Like Heaven To Me' (IASPM Working Paper 6), 1985.

Postmodernism, postmodernity

Journals such as *Cultural studies*, *New formations*, *Textual practice*, *Theory, culture and society*, and *Journal of communication inquiry* provide a forum for the liveliest academic debate on these terms. Andreas Huyssen: *After the great divide* (Macmillan, London, 1988) is a collection of some of the work of one of the most astute essayists in this field. For provocative work at its furthermost edge, see Arthur and Marilouise Kroker (eds): *Body invaders* (Macmillan, London, 1988), and Arthur Kroker and David Cook: *The postmodern scene* (second edition, Macmillan, London, 1988). For Jean Baudrillard, see his idiosyncratic account of what he did on his holidays in *America* (Verso, London, 1988) and Mark Poster (ed): *Jean Baudrillard; selected writings* (Polity

Press, Oxford, 1988). For Jean-François Lyotard, see the interviews in *Just gaming* (Manchester University Press, Manchester, 1987), and his account of *The postmodern condition* (Manchester University Press, Manchester, 1986) as well as the collection of earlier work in *Driftworks* (Semiotext(e), New York, 1984) and Geoffrey Bennington: *Writing the event* (Manchester University Press, Manchester, 1988). For Gilles Deleuze and Felix Guattari, see *On the line* (Semiotext(e), New York, 1983), and *Nomadology* (Semiotext(e), New York, 1986). For different, mainly Australian emphases, see Andre Frankovits (ed): *Seduced and abandoned: the Baudrillard scene* (Stonemoss, Glebe, 1984) and Meaghan Morris: *The pirate's fiancee* (Verso, London, 1988). For early 1980s formulations of the debate, see Hal Foster (ed): *Postmodern culture* (Pluto Press, London, 1985). For a collection of conference papers from 1985, see *Postmodernism* (Free Association Books, London, 1989). For other important debates, see Lawrence Grossberg: *It's a sin: essays on postmodernism, politics and culture* (Power Publications, Sydney, 1988).